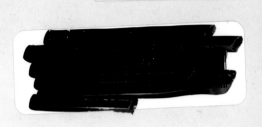

D1490701

DISCARD

A NEW SYSTEM OF READING
BASED ON THE
MATHEMATICAL THEORY OF SETS

A New System of Reading Based On The Mathematical Theory of Sets

By

WILLIAM F. KAVANAGH, A.B.

VANTAGE PRESS

NEW YORK   WASHINGTON   HOLLYWOOD

FIRST EDITION

Copyright, © 1964, by William F. Kavanagh

Published by Vantage Press, Inc.
120 West 31st Street, New York 1, N.Y.

Manufactured in the United States of America

To
Monongahela

Suffer the little children to come unto me, and do not hinder them, for such is the kingdom of God.

Amen, I say unto you, if you do not become as little children you shall not enter the kingdom of heaven.

Saint Mark. 10, 13-16

To
Monongahela

Suffer the little children to come unto me, and do not hinder them, for such is the Kingdom of God. Amen, I say unto you, if you do not become as little children you shall not enter the Kingdom of heaven.

— Saint Mark, 10, 13-16

(omit)

LESSON I

As in the Mathematical Theory of Sets we begin with a basic set of objects of our perception or of our thought, which are called *elements* of the set. In the case of the English language, the set consists of the basic sounds and the letters of the alphabet as we know them from childhood; plus the five short vowels we will use in this system of reading.

Therefore we have:

A,B,C,D,E,F,G,H,I,J,K,L,M,N,O,P,Q,R,S,T,U,V,W,X,Y,Z, plus five short vowels:

A as in at, cat, mat, sat; E as in Ed, bed, red, wed; I as in it, sit, sin, ill, crib; O as in on, lot, not, rob; U as in up, but, sun, sub.

Repeating the set, we have, to begin our system of reading: A,B,C,D,E,F,G,H,I,J,K,L,M,N,O,P,Q,R,S,T,U,V,W,X,Y,Z, AND the FIVE and *only* five—SHORT VOWELS as indicated above.

Now the use of only five short vowels may appear to be rather radical. And it is. What we do is *eliminate the formal teaching* of the great variety of short vowels. And it is our purpose to show that a thorough knowledge of the Set as indicated above will suffice to enable the student and the non-reader to read. We will, of course, arrive at the short vowels other than those in the set in another way, which will be explained in the next few pages. But the reader will see that if we can derive a system of teaching reading which eliminates the great variety of short vowels, and if that system works—and the author has seen it work—we have taken a giant step towards the simplification of the teaching of reading.

The reader will find that I have changed the names of four letters of the alphabet. The reason for these changes is that the present names do not contain the sounds of the letters as they are used in words; and that as now named they have little relation to present-day use, and consequently are confusing to the student.

11

The four letters are: **H, Q, W** and **Y**. The new names are: **He**, as in **He** is my brother; **Qui**, as in **Qui-et**; **We** as in **We** are mortals; and **Ye** (the old form of the personal pronoun *You*). This changing of the names of these letters is not necessarily vital to the system here outlined; but it would be desirable to use these names when teaching children the alphabet in the first grade. Lessons,

The next idea the reader should keep in mind is that the elimination of the teaching of the vast variety of short vowels is based on the fact that as any parent or teacher knows who has heard children recite in a school play, children do not place the accents on words correctly when they speak. So we hear them address an audience thus:

FATH ERS AND MOTH ERS AND LA DIES AND GEN TLE MEN . . . —that is, THEY ACCENT EACH AND EVERY SYLLABLE.

This is also true of people who have difficulty in the beginning stages of learning a language. An Indian on an old television program is often portrayed as having this habit of accenting each syllable. So we hear him recite his woes of betrayal to the new Marshall from Washington come West to bring Law and Order. The Indian Chief says:

WHITE MAN SPEAK WITH FORK'D TONGUE. LIE TO RED MAN. . . .

The Indian, unfamiliar with the language he is speaking, also accents all the syllables for fear of making a mistake, and because he is just not used to speaking Engish at any speed. The manner of speaking of the Indian and that of the child are the same. This is also true of the American in Paris, the Russian in New York—of all people when they speak a language with which they are unfamiliar.

Where then do accents come from? And why are accents necessary? Because in addition to the words to be pronounced there is the human machine through which these words must, as it were, be filtered. An accent comes on an exhalation of breath. And it is obvious that if we accented each syllable like the Indian or the child we would soon run out of breath. It would take longer to convey our thoughts. Since we wish to speak and at the same time save breath and conserve our strength we must use accents and using them something has to give. What gives

12

are the long and short vowels as we have learned them thus far. The other variety of short vowels come to us also because of the juxtaposition to the long or short vowels of certain letters. For example: the A in *air* should be pronounced long but the R following tends to shorten the long vowel. This is because the tongue must be forward in the mouth to pronounce the long A and towards the rear of the mouth to make the sound of R.

The author thinks then that there is little purpose in teaching the long variety of short vowels, since we will use them anyway as soon as we develop facility in reading or speaking; and the short vowels are more the result of local speech patterns than of school instruction.

To repeat: The short vowels we use are: A as in *at;* E as in *red;* I as in *it;* O as in *not;* U as in *up.* Consider why we do this: The word *abandon* is divided and accented:

a ban' don

Now the system explained in this book would divide the word differently as indicated here:

ab an don

and we would, as is shown, accent all the syllables.

What does this accomplish? Well, if we try to repeat the word *ab an don* and accent each syllable as indicated we find that it's difficult to do so, and to do so quickly. For, once we repeat these three syllables quickly . . . *ab an don* . . . we find that we are forced by our speech mechanics to arrive at the first pronunciation as it is divided in most dictionaries, namely *a ban don.* The same thing happens in the case of the other short vowels: E,I,O,U. Now, if we remember the way children—and Indians— accent every syllable, the relationship between the dictionary *a ban don* and our *ab an don* becomes obvious. The child and the Indian will also, as we do, pronounce the same word in the way most dictionaries advise, when they gain facility in speaking and reading. Therefore it is not necessary or even desirable from the point of view of simplicity TO TEACH THEM A GREAT VARIETY OF SHORT VOWELS, since it does not accomplish anything that is not accomplished naturally by the mechanics of the speech machine—the voice, the mouth, the teeth, the tongue, the lungs. And the elimination of the teaching of the variety of short vowels makes the teaching of reading much simpler. We can then construct a system of teaching reading which has some logic and reason and consistency.

The great difficulty besetting children and some adult non-readers is a result of a lack of knowledge of:

1) the sounds of the letters in the alphabet;

2) the circumstances under which the sounds of the letters of the alphabet change—for example, C becomes S when followed by E or I, G becomes a J sound when followed by E or I;

3) when the vowels are either long or short;

4) when and where to place the accents on words.

It is these four things which we will attempt to make clear in the following pages.

LESSON II

The letters of the alphabet, as indicated on page 11, will be our starting point. We now examine them with the purpose of determining their function in reading and speech. And we find that they do different things and are related in their function to specific parts of the speaking mechanism.

Going through the alphabet we see that there are five letters called vowels. They are: A E I O U. The vowels are like the vocal chords without which a man couldn't speak or make any sounds. If a human being loses his vocal chords because of an operation, he, in a sense, loses the vowels: A E I O U. He loses the vowels; while still retaining the other letters which are formed by the lips, mouth, tongue, and teeth. It is possible, then, to have a complete sound, syllable, or word *only* when we have the help of the vowels, either long or short: *a man, I am, E ven, o pen.* But it is NOT POSSIBLE to have a complete sound, syllable or word without the vowels, any more than a man can speak without vocal chords.

In the next few pages we will begin to build a series of one- and two-letter syllables from which we will derive some rules which will become the essential principles of this system of reading.

Let us, at this point, spell the names of the letters of the alphabet as we find them spelled in words. You will note the names of some letters have been changed, as was previously explained.

a	as in	a ble
be	as in	be gum
ce	as in	Ce dric
de	as in	de cent
e	as in	e ven
ef	as in	ef fort
ge	as in	ge nius
he *	as in	he is here *
I	as in	I am
ja	as in	Ja cob
ka	as in	ka lif
el	as in	el ephant
em	as in	em pty
en	as in	en emy
o	as in	o pen
pe	as in	Pe ter
qui *	as in	qui et *
ar	as in	ar row
es	as in	es cape
te	as in	te dious
u	as in	U Thant, U kulele, u nit,
ve	as in	Ve nus

16

we *	as in	we are *
ex	as in	ex pect
ye *	as in	ye morals *
ze	as in	ze bra

From an analysis of the above list of the names of the letters of alphabet as they are used in words; we discover three rules which will aid us to simplify the teaching of reading. We find that if the vowel stands alone it is long: A as in *a-ble;* E as in e-ven; I as in I am; O as in *o-pen;* U as in *u-sual.* In the case of e,u we make no distinction between a long u and e,u. So in a word like *oc*-u-*list* the u stands alone, and is therefore pronounced long.

We find also that in a two-letter syllable, if the vowel is *first,* it is pronounced short: EF as in *ef-fort,* EN as in *en-em-y,* etc. And finally we find that if a vowel in a two-letter syllable is second, it is pronounced long: KA as in *ka-lif;* PE as in *Pe-ter;* ZE as in *ze-bra.*

From this analysis we derive some simple rules which form one of the essential points and the basic principle of this system of reading.

To these rules we give names which are merely intended (1) to be an aid to remembering the rule, (2) are examples of the rules. They have no other significance.

1) *The I Go Up rule*

a) If a vowel stands alone forming a syllable; it is pronounced long (I as in *I* am, *I go up;* O as in *o-ver;* E as in *e-ven;* A as in a-ble).

b) If a vowel is second in a two letter syllable; the vowel is long (I GO up; and, from the words in the chart on page— BE: *be-gum;* CE: *Ce-dric;* DE: *de-cent;* GE: *ge-nius;* HE: *he*

---

* the letters **H, O, W, Y,** have new names, as explained on page —.
** When two letters are separated by a comma; it means they should both be pronounced long and separately.

was; JA: *Ja-cob;* KA: *ka-lif;* PE: *Pe-ter;* QUI: *qui-et;* TE: *te-dius!*
VE: Ve-nus; WE: *we are;* YE: *ye mortals;* ZE: *ze-bra*).

c) If a vowel is first in a two letter syllable; it is pronounced short. (EF: *ef-fort;* EL: *el-ephant;* EM: *em-pty;* EN: *en-em-y;* AR: *ar-rant;* es: ES-*cape;* ex: EX*pect*)

2) The Slo rule

a) If a vowel ends a syllable of three or more letters, it is long (*sla-very; pre-vious; tri-cycle; pro-noun; in-flu-en*ce).

3) The Egg rule

a) If a vowel is at the beginning of a three-letter syllable; the vowel is short (add, egg, ill, odd).

4) The Tom Left His Golf Clubs Here rule

a) If a vowel is in the middle of a syllable or a word of three, four, or more letters, the vowel is *short, three letters*: Tom, his, *also* cat, set, sit, not, but; *four letters*: left, golf, bath, sled, this, clot, putt; *five and six letters*: clubs stands smash, slept, smock, ducks, thrill).

Note: THE MOST IMPORTANT RULE above is the *I GO UP* rule. The others, as you can see, can be derived from it.

5) The BOAT rule

If, in a syllable or word of two, three, four or five letters, one vowel is followed immediately by a second vowel, the second vowel makes the first vowel *long* (aim, meat, toe, suit; *also,* claim, clean float, flue).

Using the rules we've just mentioned we will now write out the alphabet ten times; putting the five vowels after each letter of the alphabet and then putting the five vowels before each of the letters. Then we will pronounce the resulting syllables according to the rules we have just learned.

The parent or the teacher using this system to teach reading to children should keep in mind that this system cannot be digested all at once. But the teacher, and especially the parent, can do much to drill the TEN NEW ALPHABETS which follow even before the child reaches school age. Even the very young can learn and remember to recite these sounds if they are taught them with the same sing-song manner they now learn to recite the alphabet. Of course, a preschool child is too young to burden with the complete explanation of how this system works. No wise parent or teacher would make that error.

In listing the sounds for what I call the NEW ALPHABETS I have placed after them some words which are to serve as a pronunciation key. It is well to remember that the only vowels I intend to use are: a e i o u, the long vowels; and a e i o u, the short vowels.

Keep in mind, while reading and trying to pronounce the TEN NEW ALPHABETS, that in a two-letter syllable, if the vowel is *first* it is *short;* and if the vowel is *second* it is *long.* Where we have a two-letter syllable made up of two vowels, the second vowel tells us that the first is long, and the second is silent. There are some situations where two vowels have their own special sound (*aa; i, a; u, a; oi; oy; a, o; au; e, u; i, u; i, o;*). The pronunciation of these combinations is given in the following pages. In learning the New Alphabets it is not necessary for the beginning student to learn the words in the pronunciation key in the right hand column. It is enough the child learn the sounds of the New Alphabets in the left hand column. The pronunciation key is for the teacher and the parent or the adult helping the child.

New Alphabet Number One

The letter A is placed *after* each letter of the old alphabet

aa *	as in	Baa, Baa, black sheep
ba	as in	ba by
ca	as in	ca dence
da	as in	Da vid
ea	as in	eat, beat, heat
fa	as in	fa tal, fa vor
ga	as in	ga ble
ha	as in	ha ven
i, a *	as in	Ind ia
ja	as in	Ja cob
ka	as in	ka lif
la	as in	la bor
ma	as in	ma jor
na	as in	na val, na tal,
oa	as in	oats, coat, boat
pa	as in	pa tron, pa per
qua	as in	Qua ker
ra	as in	ra dio, ra diant
sa	as in	Sa viour, sa ble, sa bei
ta	as in	ta ble, ta bor
u, a *	as in	ac qua

va	as in	va cation
wa	as in	wa ger
xa	as in	za-ny (when an X is first, it sounds like a Z. There is no word beginning with X to illustrate this rule.)
ya	as in	Ya-ger a proper name, variation of Jaeger
za	as in	za-ny

New Alphabet Number Two

The letter E is placed *after* each letter of the old alphabet.

ae	as in	alumnae
be	as in	be-gum, be-tween, be-lieve
ce	as in	ce-dar
de	as in	de-cent
ee	as in	eel, seen, teen, bee
fe	as in	fe-ver
ge	as in	gee, ge-nius, ge-nial
he	as in	He-brew
ie	as in	chief, be-lief
je	as in	jee, Jes-us, jeep
ke	as in	ke-tone, ke-to, keep, keen, key
le	as in	le-gal, le-ver

---

* The letter combination *aa; i, a;* and *ua* have their own special sounds which must be memorized.

me	as in	me, me-ander, me-dia, me-teor
ne	as in	ne-ophyte, same sound as knee
oe	as in	toe, woe
pe	as in	Pe-ter, pe-nal
que	as in	queen, quea-sy
re	as in	re-cede
se	as in	se-cret
te	as in	te-dious
ue	as in	Sue, Tues-day
ve	as in	Ve-nus, ve-nal
we	as in	we are here, weed
xe	as in	xe-bec (when an X is first; it sounds like a Z sound)
ye	as in	"what fools ye mortals be"
ze	as in	ze-bra

New Alphabet Number Three

The letter I is placed *after* each letter of the old alphabet

ai	as in	aid, aim
bi	as in	bi-ble
ci	as in	ci-pher, ci-der
di	as in	di-aper, di-alect (same sound as die)
ei	as in	receive, receipt
fi	as in	fi-ber
gi	as in	gi-ant

22

hi	as in	hi-atus
ii	skip	there is no word having two *i's* in the same syllable
ji	as in	jibe
ki	as in	kite
li	as in	li-ar
mi	as in	mi-grate
ni	as in	ni-trogen
oi	as in	oil, boil, coin (same sound as in *boy, toy*)
pi	as in	pi-ous, pi-lot, pi-oneer, Pi-late
qui	as in	qui-et
ri	as in	ri-ot, ri-val
si	as in	Si-amese, Si-mon
ti	as in	ti-ger, ti-ny
ui	as in	suit
vi	as in	vi-tal, vi-tamin
vi	as in	wi-der
xi	as in	Zi-on (when an X is first it sounds like a Z sound)
yi	as in	a Y sound as in Yes, plus a long I sound.
zi	as in	Zi-on

New Alphabet Number Four

The letter O is placed *after* each letter of the old alphabet

a,o	as in	Na-o-mi, ba-o-bab; the a and o are both pronounced long, and separately.

23

bo	as in	bo-gy, Bo-hemia
co	as in	co-hesive, co-operate
do	as in	do-nut, do-nor
e,o	as in	E,o lian; both the e and the o are pronounced long and separately
fo	as in	foe, fo-lio, focal
go	as in	go, go-cart
ho	as in	ho-ly, ho-kum, hole, hoe, home
i,o	as in	fol-io, rat-io; the i here sounds like a long e; pronounce the e,o separately
jo	as in	Jo-el, Jo-nah, same as Joe
ko	as in	Ko-ran, Ko-dak
lo	as in	lo-cal, lo-tion
mo	as in	mo-tion, mo-tor
no	as in	no, no-tion, No-ah
oo	as in	too, moon, fool, tool
po	as in	po-et, po-dium, po-lar
quo	as in	quo-tient
ro	as in	ro-ver, Ro-man
so	as in	so-dium, so-cial
to	as in	To-bias, To-jo, to-tal
uo	as in	quote same sound as woe
vo	as in	vo-cal, vo-cabulary
wo	as in	wo-ven, Wo-den,
xo	as in	Zo-diac, (when an X is first; it sounds like a Z)

| yo | as in | yo-del, yo-ga, yo, slang for *yes*. yo-yo |
| zo | as in | Zo-diac, zo-ology. |

New Alphabet Number Five

The letter U is placed *after* each letter of the old alphabet

au	as in	pause, because, clause
bu	as in	Bu-ick
cu	as in	cu-pid
du	as in	du-ty
eu	as in	Eu-phrates
fu	as in	fu-el, fu-tile, fu-sion
gu	as in	gu-bernatorial
hu	as in	hu-man, hu-midity,
i,u	as in	you, same sound as *Yu*-goslavia; sounds like a short i plus a long u
ju	as in	Ju-piter
ku	as in	Ku-do, Ku Klux Klan
lu	as is	lu-bricate, lu-na, lu-minate
mu	as in	mu-sic, mute, mule
nu	as in	nu-cleus, nu-meral
ou	as in	though, dough
pu	as in	pu-ny, pu-nitive
quu	skip	there is no word having this syllable.
ru	as in	ru-in

su	as in	su-per
tu	as in	tu-ition
vu	as in	same sound as voo in voodoo
wu	as in	same sound as woo, to woo a bride
xu	as in	Zu-lu (when an X is first; it sounds like a Z sound.)
yu	as in	Yu-goslavia
zu	as in	Zu-lu

Note: When a long U follows the letters *b, c, f, h, m, p,* what sounds like a long E is usually inserted before the U. In other combinations of letters this extra sound is regularly omitted. However, it must be inserted after the six letters mentioned: Buick, cute, fuel, huge, music, puny. Sometimes also after D (duty) and L (lucid)

New Alphabet Number Six

The letter A is placed *before* each letter of the old alphabet

aa	as in	Baa, baa, black sheep
ab	as in	ab-dicate, ab-bot
ac	as in	ac-tion ac-robat
ad	as in	ad-jective, ad-verb
ae	as in	al-um-nae
af	as in	af-fluence, Af-rica
ag	as in	ag-onize, ag-gravate
ah	as in	ah, an expression of regret, contempt, delight
ai	as in	aim, ai-lanthus, aid

aj	as in	ag-itate (*aj* sounds like *ag* followed by *e* or *i*)
ak	as in	ak-kad (*ac*, *ak* and *aq* are all the same sound)
al	as in	al-bacore, al-bum
am	as in	am-ber, am-azon
an	as in	an-alyze, an-archist
a,o	as in	ba-o-bab, Na-o-mi; pronounce both *a* and *o* long and separately
ap	as in	ap-ple, ap-petite, ap-athy
aq	as in	aquaplane; *aq*, *ac*, *ak* have the same sound.
ar	as in	ar-row, ar-rant
as	as in	as-ter, as-pen, as-teroid
at	as in	at, at-las, at-mosphere, at-om
au	as in	pause, be-cause, Au-gust
av	as in	av-erage, av-alanche, av-id
aw	as in	aw-ful, law, draw
ax	as in	ax, ax-is, ax-iom; when an *x* is within a word it sounds like *ks*
ay	as in	may, hay, day, bay
az	as in	Az-tec, az-imuth

New Alphabet Number Seven

The Letter **E** is placed *before* each letter of the old alphabet

ea	as in	eat, beat, wheat
eb	as in	eb-ony

27

ec	as in	ec-stacy, ec-toplasm
ed	as in	Ed-ward, ed-itor
ee	as in	eel, seen, teen
ef	as in	ef-figy, ef-fort
eg	as in	egg, eg-lantine
eh	as in	*eh!* (interjection, an expression of inquiry) a short *e* plus an exhalation of breath
ei	as in	ei-ther, receipt
ej		rhymes with edge, hedge, ledge
ek	as in	ec-zema, ec-stasy, same sound as *ec* above
el	as in	el-bow, el-ement, el-evator
em	as in	em-pty, em-bassy, em-ber.
en	as in	en-emy, en-joy, en-dow
e,o	as in	Leo (both letters are pronounced long and separately.)
ep	as in	ep-ic, ep-itaph, ep-igram
eq	as in	the same sound as *ec* and *ek* above
er	as in	er-rand, er-ror, er-ratic
es	as in	es-cape, es-calator, es-tate
et	as in	et-cetera, et-ymology
eu	as in	Eu-clid, Eu-ropean, few
ev	as in	ev-er, ev-idence, ev-olution
ew	as in	flew, dew, few same sound as *eu* above, rhymes with you.

ex	as in	ex-ercise, ex-pect, ex-change (within a word X is pronounced like *ks*)
ey	as in	they, abeyance, same sound as *a* long.
ez	as in	Ezra (proper name)

New Alphabet Number Eight

The letter I is placed *before* each letter of the old alphabet

ia	as in	Ind-ia, Sylv-ia,
ib	as in	Ib-sen, crib, fib, *ad lib*
ic	as in	com-ic, ital-ic
id	as in	id-iot, id-iomatic, id-iom
ie	as in	chief, relief (same sound as *e* long)
if	as in	"If I Were King" fifty, gift, jiffy
ii	Skip	there is no word which has a double *i* in the same syllable
ij		rhymes with ridge
ik		same sound as *ic* above
il	as in	Il-iad, il-legal, ill
im	as in	im-age, im-press
in	as in	in-ability, in-dex
i,o	as in	iodine, iota
ip	as in	*ip-so facto* (hip, sip, ship)
iq		same sound as *ic* and *ik* above

29

ir	as in	ir-ritate, ir-regular, ir-ruption
is	as in	miss, Is-cariot, Is-lam, his-tory
it	as in	it, sit, lit
iu		rhymes with the pronoun *you*, sounds like a short *i* and a long *u*
iv	as in	give, live, Liv-er
ix	as in	fix, six, ix-ion (when an *X* is within a word it sounds like *ks*)
iz	as in	is, his, ris-en

New Alphabet Number Nine

The letter O is placed *before* each letter of the old alphabet

oa	as in	oats, oak
ob	as in	ob-ject, ob-ligate
oc	as in	oc-tave, oc-cupant, oc-cident
od	as in	odd, rhymes with cod, rod
oe	as in	toe, hoe
of	as in	of-fer, of-ten, of-fend
og	as in	Og-den, log, cog
oh	as in	oh, ohm, same sound as a long *o*
oi	as in	oil, coin, soil, rhymes with boy, **top**
oj		rhymes with hodgepodge, lodge
ok		same sound as *oc* in oc-cupant above
ol	as in	ol-ive, ol-igarchy, tol-erate

om	as in	om-elet, om-nibus, rhymes with Tom, bomb
on	as in	on, don, yon-der
oo	as in	boom, tool, fool
op	as in	op-era, op-erate
oq		see *oc, ok,* above (same sound as *oc* in oc-cupant)
or	as in	or-bit, or else
os	as in	os-prey, os-cillate
ot	as in	ot-ter, ot-toman, cot, dot
ou	as in	though, dough (same sound as as a long *o*)
ov		same sound as the preposition *of*
ow	as in	(same sound as a long *o*) own, low, know
ox		ox-ygen, ox-idize (when an *x* is within a word it sounds like *ks*)
oy	as in	oy-ster, boy (same sound as *oi* above)
oz	as in	Oz, the Wizard of Oz

New Alphabet Number Ten

The letter U is placed *before* each letter of the old alphabet

ua	as in	aqua
ub	as in	tub, sub, scrub
uc		rhymes with luck, stuck
ud	as in	ud-der—rhymes with mud, cud
ue		rhymes with sue, new, due, cue

uf	as in	suf-fix — rhymes with enough, rough
ug	as in	ug-ly
uh		the sound of *u* short plus an exhalation of breath
ui	as in	suit (same sound as *ue* above)
uj		rhymes with judge, smudge
uk		same sound as *uc* above— rhymes with luck
ul	as in	ul-cer, Ul-ster
um	as in	um-brage, um-brella
un	as in	un-der, un-necessary, Hungary
uo	as in	quote (same sound as woe)— rhymes with go, know, toe
up	as in	up, up-grade, up-land, sup-per, cup
ur	as in	ur-ban, ur-gent
us	as in	us, (pronoun) luster, bus
ut	as in	ut-ter, ut-most
uu		no word with *uu*
uv		rhymes with love, above
uw		no word with *uw*
ux	as in	ux-or, lux (rhymes with ducks) An *X*, final or within a word, sounds like *ks*
uy	as in	buy, guy (same sound as a long *i*)
uz	as in	fuzz, buzz (rhymes with does, Duz)

When Admiral Farragut steered through the scattered wrecks and hostile mine fields at Mobile Bay, his determined command and battle cry was: "Damn the Torpedoes. Full speed ahead." In charting a clear course through the non-reader's shoally sea of confusion, keeping the focal point of view of the child, we adopt a similar attitude of mind saying: "Forget the exceptions. Remember the rules." We therefore write some useful rules to guide us,—'rules of thumb'—which aid us in bringing a measure of order and consistency to the teaching of reading. And while no claim is made as to the percentage of times the following rules work—it is enough to say they are effective MOST OF THE TIME—and we leave the exact percentage of their effectiveness to the statistically inclined to calculate; but it is vital to a successful teaching of reading to avoid the current disastrous idea that every English word is a sort of Chinese pictograph which must be learned separately and spoon fed one by one agonizingly by the teacher.

In the beginning we said we were going to use only the five long vowels as indicated in the alphabet and five short vowels as previously mentioned. Now we consider certain letter formations which for the purposes of this system of reading we view as Equivalent Long Vowel Sounds.

The sound of the long vowel A is gotten under a variety of spellings. A as in a-ble; *ai* as in aim; *ay* as in may; *ey* as in they; *eig* as in reign; *ei* followed by n, *ei*(n), as in rein; *eigh* as in eight. So when we see *a*, *ai*, *ay*, *ey*, *eig*(n), *ei*(n), and *eigh*, in words as indicated above we will pronounce a long A sound.

The long *e* sound can be gotten in the following letter formations. *e* as in e-ven; *ee* as in eel, teen, see; *ea* as in sea, team, defeat; *ei* as in receipt; *ie* as in chief; *y* as in slow ly, holy; *i* as in Hawaii. Note—A *y* and an *i* at the end of a word sound like long *e* sounds.

*( ) *ei* when followed by an n has the sound of a long *a*.

33

** Whenever *ei* or *ie* is in a word it is pronounced like a long *e*, regardless of which letter, the *e* or the *i* is first or second. The only time the *i* in *ie* is pronounced long is when it has been changed from a long *y* as in try: tried; dry: dried; dying: died. The student of etymology and philology may supply the reason why this is so. The non reader is interested in when it happens.

*** *ea* when followed by the letters *d, f, th, lth, v, sure,* is generally pronounced short Not long, as in d:dead; f:deaf; th:death; breath; lth: health; wealth; stealth; v:heaven; sure: measure, pleasure, treasure. Exceptions: Words like: heathen, beaver, cleaver, heave, lead (present tense) bead, breathe, sheath, beadle follow the original rule that *ea* is pronounced like a long *e*. When *ea* is followed by *d, f, th, lth, v,* and *sure*, we should be alerted for a short *e* somewhat over fifty percent of the time. In three words the *a* is long: great, break, steak.

The long *i* sound can be found in the following letter formations. *i* as in I am; *i* ambic; *igh* as in sigh, sight, might; *y* as in dynamite, cyanide, try, my, . . . a *y* at the end of the first syllable of a word is pronounced like a long *i*. *ie* as in died, tried, dried etc., when a *y* at the end of the first syllable of a word has been changed to an *i* in declining the word. *aye* as in "aye, aye sir." *Eye* as in the human eye. *aisl* as in aisle. Also *ind* as in kind, find, mind. *I* is also long followed by an *ld* in the same syllable: mild, wild, child. In children, wilderness, the *i* is short. But we would syllabilize the words: chil dren, wil der ness, so that *ld* is not in the same syllable, and then we follow our rules.

The long *o* may be gotten in the following equivalent spellings. *o* as in o ver. *ou* as in though. *ow* as in low. *oe* as in toe. *oa* as in coat. *ough* as in thorough, *oh* as in "Oh, what a beautiful morning" *O(ld)* as in told, bold, sold, *o(lt)* as in bolt, *o(st)* as in most, host, exception: lost, cost. *o(ll)* as in toll. Note * the parenthesis after *O(ll), o(ld), o(lt)* means that we have a long *o* sound when *o* is followed by *ll, ld, lt,* and forms one syllable. In words like doll, loll, the long *o* seems muffled by the d and the l before the *oll*.

It will be of help to the student or child at home who has

34

some difficulty trying to distinguish between the sound of *ou* in out, found etc., and though; or between *ow* as in low and cow, to treat both for the present as long *o*'s. *Ow* and *ou* should be pronounced as long *o*'s. Anything else is an exception; we will devise some rules to govern this in the next few pages.

The long *U* sound is gotten as follows. *Eu* as in Eu phrates. *U* as in use, act u al, U Thant, u kulele, *you* as in the personal pronoun You; *yoo* as in yoo hoo, a call or greeting; *ui* as in suit; *ue* as in sue, due, Tuesday; *Yu* as Yu goslavia.

Some Rules of Thumb

The name of the Rule is an example of what the rule states. So if the student memorizes the name of the Rule he will remember the Rule.

1) The *Bike* rule:

If a word ends with the letter *E* and is separated from another vowel by a single consonant, the final *E* tells us that the first vowel is pronounced long: *bike*, late, mete, like, note, flute. (The final *E* is silent)

2) The *Georgia* rule:

If the letter G is followed by an E, an I or a Y, the G sounds like J: *Georgia*, Gym, ginger, Eugene, etc.

Note: Among the exceptions to this rule are the words give, girl, get, gear, geese, girdle. Most of them are of Anglo-Saxon (from Germani) origin, neither of which had a soft G, and have retained their original form.

3) The *Ice* and *Accident* rule:

The letter C usually sounds like a K (which is also the sound of Q) but, if followed by an E, an I, or a Y, the C is pronounced like an S as in the words *ice* and *accident*: city, ceiling, cymbal.

4) The *Yesterday a Typical* Texas *Cyclone* Hit *Swiftly* rule:

    a) When a Y begins a word it is pronounced like the Y in YE, YONDER, YESTERDAY.

    b) In the middle of a syllable, as in TYpical and chloro-PHYLL, Y sounds like a SHORT I.

    c) At the end of the first syllable of a word, Y is pronounced like a LONG I: CY clone, DY namic, MY, TRY, DY ing, WHY, etc.

d) A Y at the end of an adverb sounds like a LONG E: slowLY, quickLY, swiftLY, etc.

e) A Y at the end of a verb sounds like a LONG I: fortiFY, cruciFY, ediFY, etc.

5) The *Chrome* rule:

The letters CH regularly sound as in CHURCH. But when they are followed by L, R, OL, OR, OOL, and sometimes EM and AR, the CH sounds like K: CHlorine CHrome, psyCHology, CHord, sCHool; also CHemistry, CHaracter.

6) The *Simon Was Disappointed* rule:

a) When an S begins a word it sounds like SS as in: Simon, seed, stand, sit, etc.

b) When an S ends a word it is pronounced like a Z: as, has, was, churches, peaches, is, his, gives, lives, etc.

c) When an S ends the first syllable of a word it has the SS sound as in: dis appoint, mis conduct, mis take, his tory, etc.

d) A DOUBLE S (2 S's together) also gives the SS sound, as in kiss, miss, hiss. (See a) and c) above)

e) An S is in the middle of a syllable sounds like an SS sound as in: list, mist, first, worst, moist.

f) We also get the pure SS sound with the letter formations *ce, se,* as in ice, place, purse, worse.

g) An S between two vowels is usually pronounced like Z as in: appease, please, close, etc.

7) The *William* rule:

At the beginning of the last syllable of a word the I sounds like the Y in yonder, yesterday, etc.

Will iam, Sylv i a, Ind ian, miss ion, atten tion—Also see rule 8.

8) The *Attention* rule:

The letters TION and SION ending a word are, according to all authorities, pronounced SHUN. If we spell the TION and the SION as TYON and SYON and pronounce the Y as in yes, we will find that after repeating the word ending a few times we will have come to SHUN. *Tion* or *sion* at the end of a word forms an unaccented syllable which is always subject to greater distortion from the actual spelling than an accented syllable. Try it: *tea yon*, as in *atten tea yon* (attention) *sea yon,* as in *mis sea yon* (mission)

9) The *Sound-Ouch* Rule

OU sounds like a long O in though, dough; but when it is followed by ND (sound, hound, found, around, etc.), TH (south, mouth), T (out, about, clout, shout), CH (ouch, couch, slouch) D (loud, proud), L (foul), R (hour, our, sour), the sound becomes harsher, as in *out*. (Exception: *wound*)

10) The *Low* rule:

OW sounds like a long O as in *low;* when the OW is preceded by L (low); R (row); SN (snow); T (tow); M (mow); also, blow, throw, stow.

11) The *Cow* rule:

OW sounds as in COW, when preceded by C (cow); N (now); B (bow); D (down); H (how); P (pow); V (vow); CH (chow); also, scow, DOW-JONES.

12) The *Good Book* rule:

OO usually sounds as in moon, spoon, soon, etc. But when OO is followed by the letters D and K the OO sounds almost like a short U sound, as in *good book* (took, crook, nook, cook, wood, stood, etc.).

(Exception: food.)

13) The *New True* rule:

The letter formations UE and EW are essentially the same sound and should be treated in teaching children. Examples: Lew, glue, blue, new, etc.

14) WHEN LETTERS ARE SILENT

P is silent before N—pneumonia

K is silent before N——know, knife, knee

G is silent before N——gnome

W is silent before R——wrong, write

B is silent before T——doubt

B is silent after M——bomb, comb

15) The *Trouble* rule:

The letters R and L following a long or short vowel tend to flatten and distort the vowel sound.

 Example R: are, air, there, their, care, core, cure, tour, sure, beer, hear, etc.

 L: ale, pale, sail, mail, trail, tail, stale, etc.

PART II

The Gettysburg Address which follows has been written in the left-hand column of the page and to the right is a text which explains and applies the rules you have just learned to each word of Lincoln's address.

Notes: N.A. means NEW ALPHABETS
VFS means the VOWEL (is) FIRST (and hence is) SHORT
VSL means the VOWEL (is) SECOND (and is) LONG.

1) Four
the *U* tells us the *O* is long; but a long vowel's sound is flattened when followed by an *R* sound; the *F* before keeps the *OU* from sounding like *OW*—in our, hour, sour.

2) score
the *E* tells us the *O* is long; but a long vowel's sound is flattened when followed by an *R* sound.

3) and
AN, from the New Alphabet list, plus the sound of *D*; the vowel in *AN* is first, hence is short.

4) sev-en
EV and *EN*, from the New Alphabet list—the vowels are first, hence both are short.

5) years
the *A* tells us the *E* is long; but a long vowel's sound is flattened when followed by *R*. The *S* at the end sounds like *Z*.

6) ag o
AG from the New Alphabets—the vowel is first, hence is short; *O* stands alone, hence is pronounced long.

7) our
the *O* is long when followed by a *U*; but the long *O* sound is flattened when followed by an *R*.

8) **fath ers**   the *A* is short because it is caught in between other letters; *ER* is from the New
Alphabets; the vowel is first hence is short;
the *S* sounds like *Z*.

9) **brought**   the *UGH* after the *O* tells us the *O* is long;
but the *T* following alters the *O* sound as
does also the *R* before.

10) **forth**   *OR* is from the New Alphabets—the vowel
is first, hence is short.

11) **on**   *ON* is from the New Alphabets—the vowel
first, hence is short.

12) **this**   *IS*, from the New Alphabets—the vowel is
first, hence is short; *S* has the *SS* sound.

13) **con tin ent**   *ON, IN, EN* are all from the New Alphabets—the vowels are first, hence are short.

14) **a**   the rules tell us that when a vowel stands
alone it is pronounced long. This indefinite
article *A* should be long but becomes shortened because it is not accented.

15) **new**   *EW* is from the New Alphabets—like the
long *U* sound.

16) **na tion**   *NA* is from the New Alphabets—the vowel
is second, hence is long; in *TION,* the *I* is
a *Y* sound; the *ON* is from the New Alphabets—*TYON,* run quickly together, will
finish as *SHUN.*

17) **con ceived**   *ON* from the New Alphabets—the vowel is
first, hence is short; *CEIV:* the *C* is followed by an *E,* consequently, it is pronounced like *S; EI* tells us the *E* is long;
ED is from the New Alphabets—the vowel
is first, and so is short, but since *ED* is at
the end of the word and is not accented,
the last syllable is elided in pronunciation
. and becomes conceiv'd.

18) in   *IN* is from the New Alphabets—the vowel is first, and is therefore short.

19) lib er ty   *IB* and *ER* are from the New Alphabets—the vowels are first and are therefore short; *TY*, a *Y* at the end of a word sounds like a long *E*.

20) and   *AN* is from the N.A.—the vowel is first; and is short.

21) ded ic a ted   *ED IC ED* are all from the New Alphabets—the vowels are first, hence are short; the A stands alone, hence is pronounced long.

22) to   *TO, TWO, TOO,* have the same sound but different meanings. Only *TOO* follows this system, *TO* and *TWO* are exceptions.

23) the   like the indefinite article *A, THE,* according to our rules, should be pronounced long to rhyme with he, see, free. But since articles are rarely accented, the vowel tends to be shortened or slurred.

24) prop o sit ion   *OP, IT, ON* are from the New Alphabets—the vowels are first, hence they are short. The *O* stands alone, hence it is pronounced long; the *I* in *ION* sounds like a *Y*. When *SIT* and *ION* are run together quickly as in normal speech, the correct dictionary pronunciation will result.

25) that   *AT* is from the New Alphabets; the vowel is first, hence is short.

26) all   *AL* is from the New Alphabets—the vowel is first, hence is pronounced short . . . it rhymes with pal. Here we make no distinction between words like *all* and *pal*, sounding the *a* the same way. Local custom and speech will determine the degree of difference in the pronunciation of *pal* and *all*.

27) men   *EN* is from the New Alphabets; the vowel is first, hence is short.

28) are   the *E* at the end of are tells us to pronounce the *A* long; but the *R* sound flattens the sound of the long *A*.

29) cre a ted   *RE, ED* are both from the New Alphabets. The vowel is long in *RE* because it is second; the vowel is short in *ED* because it is first. The *A* stands alone; hence is pronounced long.

30) e qual   the *E* stands alone; hence is pronounced long. *AL* is from the New Alphabets; the vowel is first; hence is pronounced short. The *QU* sounds like *KW*.

31) Now   *OW* from the New Alphabets. The *W* tells us the *O* is pronounced long. But the *OW* preceded by the *N* sound tends to make the *OW* become harder as in *OUT*.

32) we   *WE* is from the N.A. The vowel is second; therefore is pronounced long.

33) are   the *E* tells us the *A* is pronounced long. But the *R* changes and flattens the long *A*. People from Boston and New England will usually make an effort to pronounce the long vowels like this, as in: gear, hear, air, care, etc.

34) en ga ged   *EN* and *ED* are from the N.A. The vowels are first; hence are short; *GA* is also from the N.A. but the vowel is second and is therefore long. The *G* in *GED* sounds like a *J* sound; because a *G* followed by *E* or *I* is pronounced *J*. The last syllable is not accented and is pronounced on placing the accent; engag'd (without the E).

35) in   *IN* is from the N.A. The vowel is first; the vowel is short.

41

36)	a	see 14
37)	great	This word is an exception to the *EA* rule. The *E* in the *EA* should be long; but it is not. The *A* is long instead. There are three words in which this happens. They are: GREAT, STEAK and BREAK.
38)	Civ il	*IV* and *IL* are both from the N.A. The vowels are first; the vowels are short.
39)	War	*AR* is from the N.A. This word sometimes gets various pronunciations depending on what part of the country one comes from. Here we pronounce it as in the N.A., letting local custom determine the precise sound.
40)	test ing	*ES* is from the N.A. The vowel is first; the vowel is short. *IN* is from N.A. The vowel is first; the vowel is short. Try pronouncing *IN* alone; then add a hard *G* sound. You will find you create the distinctive sound of *ING*.
41)	whether	*ET* and *ER* are from the N.A. The vowels are first; the vowels are short. Add an *H*, exhale the breath after *ET* and you will get the *TH* sound.
42)	that	*AT* is from the N.A. The vowel is first; the vowel is short.
43)	nation	see 16
44)	or	*OR* is from the N.A. The vowel is first; the vowel is short.
45)	an y	*AN* is from the N.A. The vowel is first; the vowel is short; *Y* at the end of a word sounds like a long *E*.
46)	na tion	see 16
47)	so	*SO* is from the N.A. The vowel is second; the vowel is long.

48) con ceiv ed   see 17)

49) and   see 20)

50) so   see 47)

51) ded ic a ted   see 21)

52) can   *AN* is from the N.A. The vowel is first; the vowel is short.

53) long   *ON* is from the N.A. The vowel is first and is short. The *G* hard following the *ON* gives the gong sound to *ONG*.

54) en dure   *EN* is from the N.A. The vowel is first, the vowel is short. The *U* in *DURE* is long because of the *E* at the end. But the *R* flattens the sound of the long *U*.

55) We   see 32)

56) are   see 33)

57) met   *ET* is from the N.A. The vowel is first, and so is short.

58) on   see 11)

59) a   see 14)

60) great   see 37)

61) bat tle   *At* from the N.A. The vowel is first, hence, short. The *LE* in *TLE* has the affect of merely indicating that we should make a strong *L* sound: *LE*, as in little, kettle, etc., has the purpose of telling us we should make a double *L* or *LL* sound.

62) field   *IE* is from the N.A. The *E* is pronounced long.

63) of   *OF* is an exception to our N.A. And sounds like *OV* in the N.A.

64) that   see 42)

65) war.   see 39)

| 66) | We | see 32) |

67) have — the *E* tells us the vowel *A* ought to be pronounced long. But a *V* tends to shorten it, heaven, give, etc. This does not happen always, but most of the time, so that we can establish it as a rule of thumb that a *V* will shorten a long vowel preceding it.

68) come — the *E* tells us the *O* is long, though *M* tends to soften the long *O*. When a child sees words like this one he should pronounce the *O* long rather than to hesitate and stop reading to wait to be told the exact pronunciation.

69) to — see 22)

70) ded ic ate — see 21) In *ATE* the *E* at the end tells us *A* is to be pronounced long.

71) a — see 14)

72) por tion — *OR* is from the N.A. The vowel is short: because it is first; *TION* equals *TYON* *ON* is from the N.A. and the vowel is first and short. Run *TYON* together quickly and you will have the *SHUN* we are used to hearing.

73) of — see 63)

74) that — see 42)

75) field — see 62)

76) as — *AS* is from the N.A. The vowel is short because it is first. The *S* in this case sounds like a *Z* sound. An *S* at the end of a word often sounds like a *Z*. (his, has, churches, etc.)

77) a — see 14)

78) fi nal — *FI* is from the N.A. The vowel is second and is therefore long; *AL* is from the N.A.

44

and since the vowel is first it is pronounced short.

79) rest ing — *ES* is from the N.A. The vowel is first; and short; *IN* is from the N.A.; the vowel is short, because first. See 40) about the *ING* sound.

80) place — The *E* at the end tells us the *A* is long and that the *C* is sounded like an *S*. (either *E* or *I* following *C* gives it the sound of *S*.)

81) for — *OR* from the N.A. Vowel first and short.

82) those — the *E* tells us the *O* is long. The *S* sounds like a *Z*.

83) who — this is a complete exception to the rules. You can imagine, however, that a few hundred million people have changed the pronunciation from the intent of the person who originally spelled the word. The O seems to be long; but after a few hundred years we get *WHOO*. An Englishman might pronounce this with what sounds like a long *O* but with a soft delicate touch.

84) here — the *E* at the end tells us the first *E* is long. But the *R* flattens and distorts the long vowel.

85) gave — the *E* at the end tells us the *A* is long.

86) their — *EI* from the N.A. is a long *E* sound. Again the *R* distorts the long *E*.

87) lives — the *E* tells that the *I* is long. The *S* at the end of a word sounds like a *Z*.

88) that — see 42)

89) that — see 42)

90) na tion — see 16)

91)	might	the *I* followed by *GH* tells us that the *I* is long.
92)	live	though the *E* tells us the *I* should be long, it is not. So we say that in this case the *I* is short followed by the *V* (give, live, etc.). Also see 67
93)	It	*IT* is from the N.A. VFS. **
94)	is	*IS* is from N.A. VFS. the *S* sounds like a *Z* at the end of a word.
95)	al tog eth er	*AL*, *OG*, *ET*, *ER* are all from the N.A. And so VFS. **
96)	fit ting	*IT* and *IN* are from N.A. VFS. ** See 40) *re:* ING.
97)	and	see 20)
98)	prop er	*OP* and *ER* are from the N.A. VFS **
99)	that	see 42)
100)	we	see 32)
101)	should	*OU* from the N.A. tells us the *O* is long. But this is a word that over the centuries has changed its original pronunciation. The child though should rather read it aloud as a long *O* if he is in doubt. The hearing of the word in its context will then prompt him to correct his pronunciation to the usages of local custom.
102)	do	*DO* from the N.A. says that the *O* is long. This form of the verb *to do,* though, is an exception. Like the words: to, two and too we are using the same sound to indicate different spellings. So we have: do, due, dew. We spell them differently to indicate their difference, though we use the same sound for each. It's a compromise.

** *if* a VOWEL is FIRST it is SHORT

103) this.   see 12)

104) But,   *UT* is from the N.A. VFS.

105) in   see 18)

106) a   see 14)

107) lar ger   *AR* and *ER* are from the N.A., VFS. the
                   G sounds like a *J*, followed by an *E* or
                   an *I*.

108) sense,   *EN* is from the N.A., VFS. The final *SE*
                   sounds like *SS* as in *pass*.

109) we   see 32)

110) can not   *AN* and *OT* are from the N.A., VFS.

111) ded ic ate   see 21

112) we   see 32)

113) can not   see 110)

114) con se crate *ON* is from the N.A. VFS. *SE* is from the
                   N.A. The vowel is second and is therefore
                   long. The *E* at the end of crate, tells us the
                   A is pronounced long.

115) we   see 32)

116) can not   see 110)

117) hal low   *AL* is short from the N.A., VFS. The *OW*
                   is from the N.A. and is pronounced like a
                   long *O* sound.

118) this   see 12)

119) ground.   *OU* is pronounced like a long *O*. But
                   followed by the letter *N*, it becomes harsher
                   and sounds like the *OW* in *cow, now:*
                   (ground, hound, sound, etc.)

120) The   see 23)

121) brave   the *E* at the end tells us the *A* is pronounced long.

122) men,   *EN* is from N.A. VFS.

123) liv ing   *IV* and *IN* are from the N.A. See 40) *re: ING.*

124) and   see 20)

125) dead,   *EA* would ordinarily sound the *E* long. But when *EA* is followed by *D, TH, LTH, V, SURE* it is pronounced like a short *E* (dead, death, health, heaven, measure). In words like *lead* and *lead,* present and past tense, respectively, the *EA* is long in present and short in past to distinguish the tenses.

126) who   see 83)

127) have   see 67) the *E* tells us the *A* should be long. It is short. This is an exception. But it's better to have a child pronounce the *A* long correcting it later on hearing, rather than to be completely stopped.

128) strug gled   *UG* is from the N.A. VFS. The *ED* at the end becomes garbled when we accent the first syllable. And this then becomes strug gl'd.

129) here,   the *E* at the end tells us to pronounce the first *E* long. But this first *E* becomes flattened when followed by the *R*. People from Boston come very close to pronouncing the long *E* sound.

130) have   see 127)

131) con se cra ted   *ON, ED,* are from the N.A., VFS. *SE* and *RA* are from the N.A., VSL.

132) it,   *IT* is from the N.A., VFS.

48

133) far   *AR* is from the NA., VFS—*R* tends to change the sound of even a short vowel.

134) ab ove   *AB* is from N.A., VFS. the *E* at the end tells us the *O* is long but the long vowel tends to be changed by a *V* following it (love, heaven, etc.). Both syllables are accented here. You will slur into the proper pronunciation.

135) our   *OU* is from the N.A. and is pronounced like a long *O* sound. The *R* following a long vowel, again, flattens its sound.

136) poor   *OO* is from the N.A. and has its own special sound as in moon, soon, etc. Here, again followed by *R*, its sound tends to flatten.

137) pow er   *OW* is from the N.A., and is pronounced like a long *O*. But like *OU* followed by an *R* its sound becomes harsher. The first syllable is accented. The second is not. So it's pronounced: *pow'r*.

138) to   see 22)

139) add   *AD* is from the N.A., VFS. The double *D* here we can consider as superfluous.

140) or   *OR* is from the N.A., VFS. The *R* tends, as with the long vowel, to flatten the sound of the usual short vowel.

141) de tract.   *DE* is from the N.A. The vowel is second and is therefore long. *AC*, is from N.A. VFS. *C* here has the sound of *K*.

142) **The**   see 23)

143) world   *OR* is from the N.A., VFS. Like *R*, *RL* also distorts long and short vowels. So here the *R* and the *L* combine to distort the sound of the short *O*.

144)	will	*IL* is from the N.A., VFS. The double *LL* makes no change in the sound.
145)	lit tle	*IT* is from the N.A., VFS. *LE* at the end of a word is sounded simply as an *L*.
146)	note	the *O* is long because the *E* at the end tells us to make it long.
147)	what	*AT* is from the N.A., VFS. This word will get various pronunciations depending on what part of the country one comes from. Here for the purpose of aiding the child, we pronounce it with a short *A* sound.
148)	we	see 32)
149)	say	*AY* is from the N.A. and is sounded like a long *A*.
150)	here,	see 130)
151)	but	see 104)
152)	it	see 132)
153)	can	see 110)
154)	nev er	*EV* and *ER* are both from the N.A. VFS.
155)	for get	*OR* and *ET* are from the N.A., VFS. The *G* in *get* is hard, though the rules tell us that *G* followed by *E* should have the sound of *J*.
156)	what	see 147)
157)	they	*EY* sounds like a long *A* as in the N.A.
158)	did	*ID* is from the N.A., VFS.
159)	here	see 130)
160)	It	see 132
161)	is	see 94)
162)	for	*OR* is from the N.A. VFS.

50

163) the — see 23

164) liv ing, — see 124.

165) rath er, — see 187) *AT* and *ER* are from the N.A., VFS.

166) to — see 22

167) be — *BE* is from the N.A. the Vowel is second hence is long.

168) ded ic a ted — *ED, IC, ED* are all from the N.A., VFS. The *A* stands alone, hence is long.

169) here — see 130)

170) to — see 22)

171) the — see 23)

172) un fin ish ed — *UN, IN, IS, ED* are all from the N.A., VFS. The *Ed* at the end is elided because it is not accented and comes out as: *un-finish'd*

173) work — *OR* is from the N.A., VFS. The *R* and the *K* distort the sound of the short vowel *O*.

174) which — *IC* is from the N.A., VFS. But *C* followed by *H* has a special sound as in *church*. That is, *ICH* sounds like *Itch*.

175) they — *EY*, from the N.A., sounds like a long *A*.

176) who — see 83)

177) fought — *OUGH* sounds like a long *O*. But the *T* following causes us to compromise with a flatter *O* sound.

178) here — see 130)

179) have — see 127

180) thus — *US* is from the N.A., VFS.

181) far — *AR* is from the N.A., VFS. Remember an *R* can change the sound of a long and short vowel slightly.

182) so   *SO* is from the N.A. The vowel is second and is long.

183) no bly   *NO* is from the N.A., VSL. The *Y* at the end of a word sounds like a long *E*.

184) ad van ced.   *AD, AN,* and *ED* are from the N.A., VFS. The last syllable is elided when we accent the word. Therefore we get: *advanc'd.* The *C* sounds like an *SS* followed by *E*.

185) It   see 132)

186) is   see 94)

187) rath er   *AT* and *ER* are from the N.A., VFS. The *TH* sound may be considered a special sound which must be learned separately.

188) for   *OR* from the N.A. VFS.

189) us   see 180)

190) to   see 22)

191) be   see 167)

192) here   see 130)

193) ded ic a ted   see 168)

194) to   see 22)

195) the   see 23)

196) great   see 37)

197) task   *AS* is from the N.A., VFS.

198) re main ing   *RE* is from the N.A., VSL. *AI* is from the N.A. and sounds like a long *A. IN* is from the N.A. VFS. See 40) *re ING.*

199) be fore   *BE* is from the N.A., VSL. The *E* in *FORE* tells us the *O* is long; but the *R* flattens the sound of the long *O*.

200) us   see 180)

201) that   see 42)

202) from   *OM* is from the N.A., VFS.

203) these   The *E* at the end tells us the first *E* is pronounced long. The *S* sounds like a *Z*.

204) hon or ed   *ON, OR, ED*, are all from the N.A., VFS. The last syllable is elided when we accent the word *honor'd*.

205) dead   see 126)

206) we   see 32)

207) take   the *E* at the end tells us the *A* is long.

208) in crea sed   *IN, EA*, and *ED* are from the N.A. The last syllable is elided when we accent the word as in the dictionary. It then becomes: *increas'd*.

209) de vo tion   *DE* and *VO* are from the N.A., VSL. *ON* is from N. A., VFS. *tion—tyon—shun*.

210) to   see 22)

211) that   see 42)

212) cause   *AU* is from the N.A., and has its own special sound. The *S* sounds like a *Z*.

213) for   see 188)

214) which   see 173)

215) they   see 157)

216) gave   The *E* tells us to pronounce the *A* long.

217) the   see 23)

218) last   *AS* is from the N.A., VFS.

219) full   *UL* is from the N.A., VFS.

220) mea sure   *EA* from the N.A. regularly sounds like a long *E*. But, followed by *SURE* it becomes

short. The *U* in *SURE* is long because of the *E* at the end, but followed by *R* its sound is flatter; *S* is pronounced like *Z*.

221) of   see 63)

222) de vo tion   see 209)

223) that   see 42)

224) we   see 32)

225) here   see 130)

226) high ly   *IGH* sounds like a long *I*. The *Y* at the end sounds like a long *E*.

227) re solve   *RE* is from the N.A., VSL. *OL* is from N.A., VFS.

228) that   see 42)

229) these   see 203)

230) dead   see 126)

231) shall   *AL* is from the N.A., VFS.

232) not   *OT* is from the N.A., VFS.

233) have   see 67 and 126

234) died   *EI* and *IE*, as in receive and chief are usually pronounced like a long *E*, regardless of whether the *E* or the *I* is first or second. However in words like try: tried, dry: dried, dying; die, when the *I* has been changed from a long *Y* sound the *I* is long

235) in   see 35)

236) vain   *AI* from the N.A. sounds like a long *A*.

237) that   see 42)

238) this   see 12)

239) na tion,   see 16)

240) un der   *UN*, and *ER* are both from the N.A., VFS.

241) God,   *OD* is from the N.A., VFS.

242) shall   see 231)

243) have   see 127)

244) a   see 36)

245) new   *EW* is from the N.A., and *S* sounds like a long *U*.

246) birth   *IR* is from the N.A., VFS.

247) of   see 63)

248) free dom   *EE* is from the N.A., and sounds like a long *E; OM* is from the N.A., VFS.

249) and   see 20)

250) that   see 42)

251) gov ern ment   *OV, ER, EN* are all from the N.A., VFS.

252) of   see 63)

253) the   see 23)

254) peo ple,   *E* is long. The *LE* sounds like a strong *L* as in gull.

255) by   A *Y* at the end of the first syllable of a word sounds like a long *I*.

256) the   see 23)

257) peop le,   see 254)

258) for   see 188)

259) the   see 23)

260) peop le,   see 254)

261) shall   see 231)

262) not   see 232)

263) per ish   *ER* and *ISH* are from the N.A., VFS.

264) from   *OM* is from the N.A., VFS.

265) the   see 23)

266) earth   *EA*, from the N.A., tells us the *E* is long; but a long vowel followed by an *R* has its sound flattened by the *R*.

PART III

In trying to establish proof that this system of teaching reading is workable beyond his experience in the classroom, the author studied the manner in which various authorities divided words into syllables and found the vast majority of words follow this system without any rearranging of the common syllabification of the words. Listed here and in the next few pages are those words which have to be redivided in the way this system suggests. From some fifty thousand studied some two thousand are redivided, which then results in our having devised a consistent system of reading which is a logical development of the original alphabet.

Remember that the syllables on the left must all be accented in the manner of a little child or that Indian we mentioned earlier. After repeating these syllables a few times you will find it is difficult to continue to accent each syllable and, at the same time, to say the words with any speed. You then, to save breath, accent one syllable; as soon as you do this you tend to muffle the other syllables and you will have the pronunciation indicated on the right, as well as all the other short vowels we eliminated in the beginning.

It is well also to bear in mind that when syllables are run together they have what we might call a COLLISION EFFECT on each other. By this we mean that just as two automobiles have a distinct existence separate from each other when riding along the road; so do the independent syllables when they stand alone. But as the front end of a Buick, the grill, bumper, fenders, rams into the rear of a Cadillac it is no longer a "pure" Buick any more. It is shaped by the trunk of the Cadillac as the Cadillac also is shaped by the Buick. The same thing may be said, metaphorically of course, about the COLLISION EFFECT when Syllables, as it were, COLLIDE. We see that, for example in the word 'sit u a tion' after we accent or 'collide' the syllable we have 'si tu a shun. Notice the first t is no longer a "pure t." In the word *az ure* we find we have the pronunciation, according to most dictionaries, *azh-er* or *a-zher*, it is no longer a "pure" z sound. This again is because of the COLLISION EFFECT. Finally we may think in terms of another insight, that even people meeting and associating with others are no longer the same for the experience, people tending to influence and change each other in a kind of human 'colliding.'

In teaching a child to read by this system follow this procedure:

Teach the child the New Alphabets and insist upon complete mastery of them. The child must be as familiar with the New Alphabets as he is now of the standard alphabet. The New Alphabets can be taught as early as one would begin to teach the alphabets now.

After the child has mastered the New Alphabets, take the child through any standard dictionary in which the words are divided into syllables. Be careful to redivide words needing redivision as explained and illustrated in the book.

Introduce the rules; the Boat, Georgia, Bike, etc. as you go along reading the words from the dictionary. Note: It is not necessary the child know the meaning and definitions of the words he reads in the dictionary.

When the child has mastered the New Alphabets, is able to read words from the dictionary, and knows the rules we have outlined, it might be well to introduce him to some reading material books, magazine etc. The teacher and the parent should help to show how the words are divided in the reading material chosen: newspaper headlines and advertisements.

It is well to keep in mind the suggestions made here as to the procedure to be followed are just that; suggestions and must be followed with some measure of common sense if not wisdom.

A

The New System	The Standard Dictionary
Aar on	same
ab ack	a back
ab aft	a baft
ab an don	a ban don
ab ase	a base
ab ash	a bash
ab ate	a bate
ab bess	same
ab bey	same
ab bot	same
ab bre viate	ab bre vi ate
ab dic ate	ab di cate
ab do men	same
ab duct	same
A bel	same
ab er ra tion	same
ab et	a bet
ab ey ance	a bey ance
ab hor	same
ab hor rent	same
ab ide	a bide
ab il it y	a bil i ty

ab ject	same
ab jure	same
ab laze	a blaze
a ble	same
ab lu tion	same
a bly	same
ab neg ate	ab ne gate
ab nor mal	same
ab oard	a board
ab ode	a bode
ab ol ish	a bol ish
ab o lit ion	ab o li tion
ab om in ab le	a bom in ab le
ab or ig in al	ab o rig i nal
ab or tive	a bor tive
ab ound	a bound
ab out	a bout
ab ove	a bove
ab rade	a brade
A brah am	A bra ham
ab ra sive	a bra sive
ab reast	a breast
ab ridge	a bridge
ab road	a broad
ab ro gate	same
ab rupt	a brupt

ab scess	same
ab sence	same
ab sent	same
ab sen tee	same
ab sent ly	same
ab so lute	same
ab so lute ly	same
ab so lu tion	same
ab solve	same
ab sorb	same
ab sorp tion	same
ab stain	same
ab ste mious	ab ste mi ous
ab stin ence	ab sti nence
ab stract	same
ab struse	same
ab surd	same
ab surd it y	ab surd i ty
ab un dance	a bun dance
ab un dant	a bun dant
ab use	a buse
ab u sive	a bu sive
ab ut	a but
ab ut ment	a but ment
ab ys mal	a bys mal
ab yss	a byss
Ab ys sin ia	same

From this point on we list only words divided differently in the two systems. Out of some fifty thousand words we make changes in fewer than two thousand. And the changes, as you will note, are not world shaking, nor do they violate common sense.

ac ad em ic	ac a dem ic
ac a cia	a ca cia
ac ad em y	a cad e my
ac cid en tal	ac ci den tal
ac clam a tion	ac cla ma tion
ac clim ate	ac cli mate
ac cliv it y	ac cliv i ty
ac com pan im ent	ac com pa ni ment
ac coun tab le	ac count a ble
ac cur ac y	ac cu ra cy
ac cur ate	ac cu rate
ac et ate	ac e tate
ac et ic	a ce tic
ac et yl ene	a cet y lene
ach ieve	a chieve
ach ieve ment	a chieve ment
Ach il les	A chil les
ac id it y	a cid i ty
ac id o sis	ac i do sis
ac ous tic	a cous tic
ac rim o nious	ac ri mo ni ous
ac rim o ny	ac ri mo ny

ac rop o lis	a crop o lis
ac ross	a cross
ac tiv ate	ac ti vate
ac tu al it y	ac tu al i ty
ac u men	a cu men
ac ute	a cute
ad ag io	a dag io
ad am ant	ad a mant
ad apt	a dapt
ad ap tab le	a dapt a ble
ad en oids	ad e noids
ad ept	a dept (adjective)
ad eq uac y *	ad e qua cy
ad ip ose	ad i pose
Ad ir on dacks	Ad i ron dacks
ad ju dic ate	ad ju di cate
ad jus tab le	ad just a ble
ad mir ab le	ad mi ra ble
ad mir al ty	ad mi ral ty
ad mir a tion	ad mi ra tion
ad mis sib le	ad mis si ble
ad mon it or y	ad mon i tory
ad o be	a do be

---

* Note: We consider *qu* equivalent to *kw*. and separate them here in a kind of poetic license, though ordinarily they are not separated.

ad opt	a dopt
ad or ab le	a dor a ble
ad ore	a dore
ad orn	a dorn
ad rift	a drift
ad roit	a droit
ad ult	a dult
ad ul ter ate	a dul ter ate
ad ul ter y	a dul ter y
ad ver sit y	ad ver si ty
ad ver ti zing	ad ver tiz ing
ad vi sab le	ad vis a ble
ad vi sed ly	ad vis ed ly
ad vi sor y	ad vi so ry
ad vo cac y	ad vo ca cy
ae ro naut	aer o naut
ae ro nau tics	aer o nau tics
ae ro plane	aer o plane
af ar	a far
af fab le	af fa ble
af fid a vit	af fi da vit
af fin it y	af fin i ty
af firm at ive	af firm a tive
Af ghan is tan	Af ghan i stan
af ield	a field
af ire	a fire
af lame	a flame

64

af loat	a float
af ore said	a fore said
af oul	a foul
af raid	a fraid
af resh	a fresh
ag ain	a gain
Ag am em non	Ag a mem non
ag ape	a gape
ag en da	a gen da
ag grav ate	ag gra vate
ag hast	a ghast
ag il it y	a gil i ty
ag it ate	ag i tate
ag it a tion	ag i ta tion
ag low	a glow
ag o	a go
ag og	a gog
ag rar ian	a grar ian
ag ree	a gree
ag ree ab le	a gree a ble
ag ric ul ture	ag ri cul ture
ag round	a ground
aj ar	a jar
ak in	a kin
Al ab am a *	Al a bam a

* Note: The last a in Alabama tends to become short because it is not accented.

al ab as ter	al a bas ter
al ac rit y	a lac ri ty
al arm ing	a larm ing
Al as ka	A las ka
Al ban y	Al ba ny
al bat ross	al ba tross
al chem ist	al che mist
al ert	a lert
al ib i	al i bi
al ight	a light
al ign	a lign
al ike	a like
al im ent	al i ment
al im o ny	al i mo ny
al ine	a line
al ive	a live
al kal i	al ka li
al kal oid	al ka loid
al leg a tion	al le ga tion
Al leg hen ies	Al le ghe nies
al leg or y	al le go ry
al lel u ia	al le lu ia
al lig a tor	al li ga tor
al ong	a long
al oof	a loof
al phab et	al pha bet

al tern at ive	al ter na tive
al tim et er	al tim e ter
al tit ude	al ti tude
al u min um	a lu mi num
al um na	a lum na
al um nus	a lum nus
am al gam ate	a mal gam ate
am ass	a mass
am at eur	am a teur
am at or y	am a to ry
am aze	a maze
am a zing	a maz ing
am az on	am a zon
am bas sad or	am bas sa dor
am bid ex trous	am bi dex trous
am big u it y	am bi gu i ty
am bit ion	am bi tion
am e ba	a me ba
am e lio rate	a mel lio rate
am e nab le	a me na ble
am end	a mend
am end ment	a mend ment
am en it y	a men i ty
Am er ic a	A mer i ca
am eth yst	am e thyst
am ic ab le	am i ca ble

am id	a mid
am id ships	a mid ships
am iss	a miss
am mu nit ion	am mu ni tion
am ok	a mok
am ong	a mong
am or ous	am o rous
am or phous	a mor phous
am ount	a mount
am plif y	am pli fy
am plit ude	am pli tude
am uck	a muck
am use	a muse
am use ment	a muse ment
am u sing	a mus ing
an ach ro nism	a nach ro nism
an al og ous	an al o gous
an al og y	a nal o gy
an al ys is	a nal y sis
an al yze	an a lyze
an ath em a	a nath e ma
an at om ize	a nat o mize
an at om y	a nat o my
an e mia	a ne mia
an ew	a new
an im ad ver sion	an i mad ver sion

an im al	an i mal
an im ate	an i mate
an im a ted	an i ma ted
an im os it y	an i mos i ty
an im us	an i mus
an ni hil ate	an ni hi late
an niv er sar y	an ni ver sa ry
an nu it y	an nu i ty
an oint	a noint
an om al ous	a nom a lous
an om al y	a nom a ly
an on ym ous	a non y mous
an oph el es	a noph e les
an te ce dent	an te ced ent
an tel ope	an te lope
an thrac ite	an thra cite
an tic ip ate	an tic i pate
an tim o ny	anti mony
an tip ath y	an tip a thy
an tiq uit y	an tiq ui ty
an tis ep tic	an ti sep tic
anx i et y	anx i e ty
ap art ment	a part ment
ap ath et ic	ap a thet ic
ap ath y	ap a thy
ap lomb	a plomb

ap oc al ypse	a poc a lypse
Ap ol lo	A pol lo
ap ol o get ic	a pol o get ic
ap ol o gist	a pol o gist
ap ol o gy	a pol o gy
ap os tas y	a pos ta sy
ap os tate	a pos tate
ap os tle	a pos tle
ap os tro phe	a pos tro phe
ap oth ec ar y	a poth e car y
ap oth e o sis	a poth e o sis
Ap pal a chians	Ap pa la chi ans
ap par a tus	ap pa ra tus
ap pet ite	ap pe tite
ap pet i zer	ap pe tiz er
ap plic ab le	ap pli ca ble
ap plic ant	ap pli cant
ap plic a tion	ap pli ca tion
ap pos it ion	ap po si tion
ap prox im ate	ap prox i mate
ap pur ten ance	ap pur te nance
ap ric ot	a pri cot
apt it ude	ap ti tude
ar ab esque	ar a besque
Ar a bia	A ra bi a
Ar ab ic	Ar a bic

ar bit **er**	ar bi ter
ar bit **rar y**	ar bi trar y
ar bit **rate**	ar bi trate
ar bit ra **tion**	ar bi tra tion
ar bit ra **tor**	ar bi tra tor
ar e **na**	a re na
ar gu **men tat ive**	ar gu men ta tive
ar **ight**	a right
ar ise	a rise
ar is toc **rac y**	ar is toc ra cy
ar ith met **ic**	a rith me tic
Ar iz o **na**	Ar i zo na
Ar mad **a**	Ar ma da
ar mad **il lo**	ar ma dil lo
ar mam **ent**	ar ma ment
ar mis **tice**	ar mi stice
ar o **ma**	a ro ma
ar ose	a rose
ar ound	a round
ar ouse	a rouse
ar ri val	ar riv al
ar sen al	ar se nal
ar sen ic	ar se nic
ar tic le	ar ti cle
ar tif ice	ar ti fice
ar tif ic er	ar ti fi cer

ar tif ic ial	ar ti fi cial
ar tis an	ar ti san
as cor bic	a scor bic
ash amed	a shamed
ash ore	a shore
as ide	a side
as kew	a skew
as leep	a sleep
as per it y	as per i ty
as pir a tion	as pi ra tion
as sas sin ate	as sas si nate
as sim il ate	as sim i late
as tig mat ism	a stig ma tism
as tir	a stir
as tray	a stray
as tride	a stride
as un der	a sun der
as y lum	a sy lum
ath irst	a thirst
at om i zer	at om iz er
at one ment	a tone ment
at op	a top
at ro cious	a tro cious
at roc it y	a troc i ty
at tit ude	at ti tude
aud it or y	au di to ry

au ric le	au ri cle
aus ter it y	aus ter i ty
au then tic ate	au then ti cate
au then tic it y	au then tic i ty
au thor it ar ian	au thor i tar i an
au thor it y	au thor i ty
au to bi og raph y	au to bi og ra phy
au toc rac y	au toc ra cy
au tom at on	au tom a ton
au ton om y	au ton o my
av ail	a vail
av ail ab le	a vail a ble
av al anche	av a lanche
av ar ice	av a rice
av enge	a venge
av en ue	av e nue
av er	a ver
av erse	a verse
av er sion	a ver sion
av ert	a vert
av oid	a void
av ouch	a vouch
av ow	a vow
aw ait	a wait
aw are	a ware
aw a ken	a wak en

aw ard	a ward
aw ay	a way
aw oke	a woke

B

bab oon	ba boon
Bab yl on	Bab y lon
bac cal au re ate	bac ca lau re ate
bach el or	bach e lor
bac il lus	ba cil lus
bac ter ia	bac te ri a
bac ter ic ide	bac te ri cide
bac ter i,ol o gy	bac te ri ol o gy
bac ter ium	bac te ri um
ba ker y	bak er y
ba king	bak ing
bal con y	bal co ny
Bal tim ore	Bal ti more
ban an a	ba nan a
bar bar ism	bar ba rism
bar bar it y	bar bar i ty
bar bar ous	bar ba rous
bar beq ue	bar be que
bar bit u rate	bar bi tu rate
Bar cel o na	Bar ce lo na

bar nac le	bar na cle
bar om et er	ba rom e ter
bar rac u da	bar ra cu da
bar ric ade	bar ri cade
ba sal	bas al
bas alt	ba salt
bas il ic a	ba sil i ca
bay on et	bay o net
baz aar	ba zaar
be at if ic	be a tif ic
be at if y	be at i fy
be at it ude	be at i tude
bea u tif ul	beau ti ful
bel lad on na	bel la don na
bel lic ose	bel li cose
ben ef ic ent	be nef i cent
ben ef it	ben e fit
ben ev o lence	be nev o lence
ben ev o lent	be nev o lent
ben ig nit y	be nig ni ty
bib li,og raph y	bib li og ra phy
big am y	big a my
bin oc u lar	bi noc u lar
bi tu min ous	bi tu mi nous
bo ler o	bo le ro
Bol shev ik	Bol she vik

75

bon voy age	bon vo yage
bor ic ac id	bo ric acid
bot an y	bot a ny
boul ev ard	boul e vard
bound ar y	bound a ry
boun tif ul	boun ti ful
bra cing	brac ing
brai ny	brain y
brav ad o	bra va do
bra ver y	brav er y
brav o	bra vo
Braz il	Bra zil
brev it y	brev i ty
bric ab rac	bric a brac
brig ade	bri gade
broc col i	broc co li
bru tal it y	bru tal i ty
buc can eer	buc ca neer
Bu dap est	Bu da pest
buf fal o	buf fa lo
bul let in	bul le tin
bun gal ow	bun ga low

C

cab al	ca bal
cab in et	cab i net

cab oose	ca boose
cac a o	ca ca o
cad av er ous	ca dav er ous
cad et	ca det
caf et e ri,a	caf e te ria
caj ole	ca jole
cal ab ash	cal a bash
cal am it y	ca lam i ty
cal cim ine	cal ci mine
cal cu la ting	cal cu lat ing
cal ib rate	cal i brate
cal ic o	cal i co
Cal if or ni,a	Cal i for nia
cal ip er	cal i per
cal or ic	ca lor ic
Cal var y	Cal va ry
can ard	ca nard
can as ta	ca nas ta
can del ab rum	can de la brum
can did ate	can di date
can nib al	can ni bal
can on ic al	ca non i cal
can op y	can o py
can tal oupe	can ta loupe
ca pab le	ca pa ble
cap a cious	ca pa cious

cap ac it y	cap i tal
cap it al	ca pac i ty
cap it al ism	cap i tal ism
cap it ol	cap i tol
cap it u late	ca pit u late
cap rice	ca price
cap tiv ate	cap ti vate
cap tiv it y	cap tiv i ty
car av an	car a van
car aw ay	car a way
car din al	car di nal
car eer	ca reer
car ess	ca ress
car ic at ure	car i ca ture
car niv al	car ni val
car niv or ous	car niv o rous
car ouse	ca rouse
car til age	car ti lage
ca sing	cas ing
cas in o	ca si no
cas tan ets	cas ta nets
cas tig ate	cas ti gate
cat ac lysm	cat a clysm
cat ac omb	cat a comb
cat al ogue	cat a logue
cat ap ult	cat a pult

cat ar act	cat a ract
cat arrh	ca tarrh
cat as tro **phe**	ca tas tro phe
cat eg or **ic al**	cat e gor i cal
cat eg or y	cat e go ry
cath ar tic	ca thar tic
cath e **dral**	ca the dral
caul if **low er**	cau li flower
cav al ier	cav a lier
cav it y	cav i ty
cav ort	ca vort
ced il la	ce dil la
cel eb **rate**	cel e brate
cel eb rit y	ce leb ri ty
cel er it y	ce ler i ty
cel es tial	ce les tial
cell u lar	cel lu lar
cell u loid	cel lu loid
cem et er y	cem e ter y
cen tav o	cen ta vo
cen ten ar **ian**	cen te nar i an
cen ten ar y	cen te nar y
cen tig rade	cen ti grade
cen tim e ter	cen ti me ter
cen tip ede	cen ti pede
cer am ics	ce ram ics

cer e al	ce re al
cer eb el lum	cer e bel lum
cer em o ni,al	cer e mo nial
cer em o nious	cer e mo ni ous
cer em o ny	cer e mo ny
cer tif ic ate	cer tif i cate
cer tit ude	cer ti tude
chag rin	cha grin
cham e le on	cha me le on
chan del ier	chan de lier
char it ab le	char i ta ble
char it y	char i ty
chas tit y	chas ti ty
chem ic al	chem i cal
Ches ap eake	Ches a peake
Chic ag o	Chi ca go
chick ad ee	chick a dee
chlor ide	chlo ride
chlor ine	chlo rine

D

Dam as cus	Da mas cus
dam nab le	dam na ble
dan del i on	dan de li on
deb il it y	de bil i ty
de cap it ate	de cap i tate

80

dec ib el	dec i bel
de ci ded	de cid ed
dec im ate	dec i mate
de cis ion	de ci sion
dec lar a tion	dec la ra tion
de cliv it y	de cliv i ty
dec or ate	dec o rate
de cor um	de co rum
ded ic ate	ded i cate
de fic ient	de fi cient
def in ite	def i nite
de form it y	de form i ty
de if y	de i fy
de it y	de i ty
Del aw are	Del a ware
del eg a tion	del e ga tion
del et er ious	del e te ri ous
del ic ac y	del i ca cy
del ic at es sen	del i ca tes sen
de lic ious	de li cious
de mil it ar ize	de mil i tar ize
de mo bil ize	de mo bi lize
de moc rac y	de moc ra cy
dem on strab le	de mon stra ble
Dem os then es	De mos the nes
den iz en	den i zen

81

de nom in a tion	de nom i na tion
den sit y	den si ty
den tif rice	den ti frice
de plor ab le	de plor a ble
dep o sit ion	dep o si tion
de pos it or y	de pos i tor y
dep rec ate	dep re cate
dep red a tion	dep re da tion
de pri va tion	dep ri va tion
der el ict	der e lict
de ris ion	de ri sion
der iv a tion	der i va tion
de riv at ive	de riv a tive
de rog at or y	de rog a tor y
des ec rate	des e crate
de si rab le	de sir a ble
des per ad o	des per a do
des pic ab le	des pi ca ble
des tin a tion	des ti na tion
des tin y	des ti ny
des tit ude	des ti tude
des troy	de stroy
des truc tion	de struc tion
des ul tor y	des ul to ry
de ter i,or ate	de te ri o rate
de ter min a tion	de term in a tion

det on ate

det rim ent

dev el op

de vo ted

dex ter it y

di ab e tes

di ab ol ic

di ac rit ic al

di ad em

di ag on al

di ag ram

di al ect

di al ogue

di am ond

di ap er

di aph an ous

di aph ragm

di at ribe

di er es is

di et ar y

di et et ics

di et it i,an

dif fic ul ty

dig nif ied

dig nit ar y

dig nit y

det o nate

det ri ment

de vel op

de vot ed

dex ter i ty

di a be tes

di a bol ic

di a crit i cal

di a dem

di ag o nal

di a gram

di a lect

di a logue

di a mond

di a per

di aph a nous

di a phragm

di a tribe

di er e sis

di e tar y

di e tet ics

di e ti tian

dif fi cul ty

dig ni fied

dig ni tar y

dig ni ty

dil ap id a ted	di lap i dat ed
dil at or y	dil a to ry
dil em ma	di lem ma
dil ig ence	dil i gence
dil ig ent	dil i gent
dim en sion	di men sion
dim in ish	di min ish
dim in u tion	dim i nu tion
dim it y	dim i ty
di ner	din er
diph ther i,a	diph the ri a
dip lo ma	di plo ma
dip lo mac y	di plo ma cy
dir ect	di rect
dir ect ly	di rect ly
dir ec tor	di rec tor
dir ec tor y	di rec to ry
dir ig ib le	dir i gi ble
dis ab il it y	dis a bil i ty
dis ag ree ab le	dis a gree a ble
dis ag ree ment	dis a gree ment
dis ar mam ent	dis ar ma ment
dis av ow	dis a vow
dis cip line	dis ci pline
dis com fit ure	dis com fi ture
dis cour tes y	dis cour te sy

84

dis crim in ate	dis crim i nate
dis hev el ed	di shev el ed
dis hon or ab le	dis hon or a ble
dis in teg rate	dis in te grate
dis pen sar y	dis pen sa ry
dis po sal	dis pos al
dis po sit ion	dis po si tion
dis po sses	dis pos sess
dis qual if y	dis qual i fy
dis reg ard	dis re gard
dis rep u tab le	dis rep u ta ble
dis rep ute	dis re pute
dis res pect	dis respect
dis sem in ate	dis sem i nate
dis sim il ar	dis sim i lar
dis sip ate	dis si pate
dis trib u tion	dis trib u tion
div er sif y	div er si fy
div er sion	di ver sion
div er sit y	di ver si ty
div ide	di vide
div id end	div i dend
div i der	di vid er
div in a tion	div i na tion
div ine	di vine
div in it y	di vin i ty

div is ib le	di vis i ble
div i sor	di vi sor
div orce	di vorce
div ulge	di vulge
dog mat ism	dog ma tism
do mes tic ate	do mes ti cate
dom ic ile	dom i cile
dom in ance	dom i nance
dom in ant	dom i nant
dom in ate	dom i nate
dom in eer	dom i neer
dom in o	dom i no
dun gar ee	dun ga ree
du plic ate	du pli cate
du plic it y	du plic i ty
dy nam ite	dy na mite

E

ea sil y	eas i ly
eat ab le	eat a ble
eb ul lit ion	eb ul li tion
ec cen tric it y	ec cen tric i ty
ec cle sias tic al	ec cle si as ti cal
ed ib le	ed i ble
ed if ic a tion	ed i fi ca tion

ed if ice	ed i fice
ed if y	ed i fy
Ed is on	Ed i son
ed it or	ed i tor
ef fic a cious	ef fi ca cious
ef fic ac y	ef fi ca cy
ef fic ien cy	ef fi cien cy
ef fig y	ef fi gy
El dor ad o	El do ra do
el ect	e lect
el ec tion	e lec tion
el ec trif y	e lec tri fy
el ec trol ys is	e lec trol y sis
el eg ance	el e gance
el eg ant	el e gant
el eg y	el e gy
el em ent	el e ment
el ev ate	el e vate
el ig ib il it y	el i gi bil i ty
el im in ate	e lim i nate
E liz ab eth	E liz a beth
em phas is	em pha sis
em por ium	em po ri um
em u la ted	em u lat ed
em ul sif y	e mul si fy
en cyc lic al	en cyc li cal

en cy clo pe di,a	en cy clo pe di a
en em y	en e my
en ga ging	en gag ing
en gin eer ing	en gi neer ing
en gra ving	en grav ing
en ig ma	e nig ma
en li ven	en liv en
en mit y	en mi ty
en or mit y	e nor mi ty
en tit y	en ti ty
en tom ol o gy	en to mol o gy
eph em er al	e phem er al
ep ic ure	ep i cure
ep id em ic	ep i dem ic
ep id erm is	ep i der mis
ep ig lot tis	ep i glot tis
ep ig ram	ep i gram
ep il ep sy	ep i lep sy
ep il ogue	ep i logue
ep is co pac y	e pis co pa cy
ep is co pal	e pis co pal
ep it aph	ep i taph
ep ith et	ep i thet
ep it o me	e pit o me
e quin ox	e qui nox
e ra ser	e ras er

e ro sion	e ro sion
er u dit ion	er u di tion
er ys ip el as	er y sip e las
es cal a tor	es ca la tor
es cap ade	es ca pade
es ca pism	es cap ism
Es kim o	Es ki mo
es oph ag us	e soph a gus
es pec ial ly	es pe cial ly
es tim ate	es ti mate
e tern it y	e ter ni ty
eth ic al	eth i cal
eu phem ism	eu phe mism
eu than a si,a	eu tha na sia
e van gel ic al	e van gel i cal
ev er y	ev e ry
ev id ence	ev i dence
ex am in a tion	ex am i na tion
ex cav ate	ex ca vate
ex ci tab le	ex cit a ble
ex ci ting	ex cit ing
ex clam a tion	ex cla ma tion
ex cru ci,a ting	ex cru ci at ing
ex ec rate	ex e crate
ex em plar y	ex em pla ry
ex em pli fy	ex em plif y

ex hib it ion	ex hi bi tion
ex hil ar ate	ex hil a rate
ex ig en cy	ex i gen cy
ex or bit ant	ex or bi tant
ex ped ite	ex pe dite
ex pen dit ure	ex pend i ture
ex per im ent	ex per i ment
ex plan a tion	ex pla na tion
ex plic ab le	ex pli ca ble
ex po sit ion	ex po si tion
ex pos it or y	ex pos i to ry
ex tem por ize	ex tem po rize
ex ter min ate	ex ter mi nate
ex trav ag ant	ex trav a gant
ex tre mist	ex trem ist
ex tric ate	ex tri cate

F

fa bric ate	fab ri cate
fac ade	fa cade
fac e tious	fa ce tious
fac il it ate	fa cil i tate
fa cing	fac ing
fal lac y	fal la cy
fal lib le	fal li ble

90

fal sif y	fal si fy
fam il iar	fa mil iar
fam il y	fam i ly
fan at ic	fa nat ic
fan cif ul	fan ci ful
fan tas y	fan ta sy
fas cin ate	fas ci nate
fa tal it y	fa tal i ty
fath er	fa ther
fea sib le	fea si ble
fel ic it ate	fe lic i tate
fel ic it y	fe lic i ty
fem in ine	fem i nine
fer til ize	fer ti lize
fes tiv al	fes ti val
fet ish	fe tish
fic tit tious	fic ti tious
fid el it y	fi del i ty
fil ag ree	fil a gree
fil ib us ter	fil i bus ter
fin al e	fi na le
fin esse	fi nesse
firm am ent	fir ma ment
flam ing o	fla ming o
flex ib le	flex i ble
Flor id a	Flor i da

fol lic le	fol li cle
for cib le	for ci ble
for mal it y	for mal i ty
for mid ab le	for mi da ble
for tif ic a tion	for ti fi ca tion
frat ern al	fra ter nal
fu git ive	fu gi tive
ful min ate	ful mi nate
fu mig ate	fu mi gate
fun dam en tal	fun da men tal
fu ner e al	fu ne re al
fur nit ure	fur ni ture

G

gal ore	ga lore
gal osh	ga losh
gal van ism	gal va nism
gar age	ga rage
Gar ib al di	Gar i bal di
gar ris on	gar ri son
gay et y	gay et y
gaz elle	ga zelle
gel at in	gel a tin
gen er al is sim o	gen er al is si mo
gen er al it y	gen er al i ty

gen er at ive	gen er a tive
gen er ic	ge ner ic
gen er os it y	gen er os i ty
gen es is	gen e sis
gen et ics	ge net ics
gen it ive	gen i tive
ger a nium	ge ra ni um
Ger man y	Ger ma ny
ger mic ide	ger mi cide
ger min ate	ger mi nate
Geth sem an e	Geth sem a ne
glo bal	glob al
glor if y	glo ri fy
glos sar y	glos sa ry
glu ten	glut en
gor il la	go ril la
Gran ad a	Gra na da
gran ar y	gran a ry
grat if y	grat i fy
gra ting	grat ing
gra ven	grav en
grav it a tion	grav i ta tion
grav it y	grav i ty
gren ad ier	gren a dier
grim ace	gri mace
gu ber nat or i,al	gu ber na to ri al

gui dance   guid ance

gul lib le   gul li ble

gym na sium   gym na si um

H

hab it u al   ha bit u al

hal ib ut   hal i but

hand ic raft   hand i craft

hand wri ting   **hand writ ing**

Han nib al   Han ni bal

har mon ic a   **har mon i ca**

harp sich ord   harp si chord

hel ic op ter   **hel i cop ter**

her ed it ar y   he red i tar y

hex am et er   hex am e ter

hi er o glyph ic   hier o glyph ic

his tam ine   his ta mine

his tor ic al   his tor i cal

hol id ay   hol i day

ho mic ide   hom i cide

hom il y   hom i ly

hom in y   hom i ny

ho mog en ize   ho mog e nize

hor iz on tal   hor i zon tal

hor rib le   hor ri ble

94

hor rif y	hor ri fy
hor tic ul ture	hor ti cul ture
hos pit ab le	hos pi ta ble
hos til it y	hos til i ty
hul lab al oo	hul la ba loo
hu man it y	hu man i ty
hu mid it y	hu mid i ty
hu mid or	hu mi dor
hu mil it y	hu mil i ty
hur ric ane	hur ri cane
hy ac inth	hy a cinth
hy drom et er	hy drom e ter
hy poc ris y	hy poc ri sy
hys ter ic al	hys ter i cal

I

i cic le	i ci cle
i cing	ic ing
i den tic al	i den ti cal
i den tif y	i den ti fy
id i,o syn cras y	id i o syn cra sy
il leg it im ate	il le git i mate
ill fa ted	ill fat ed
il log ic al	il log i cal
il lu min ate	il lu mi nate

95

il lus trat ive	il lus tra tive
im ag in nab le	i mag i na ble
im bec ile	im be cile
im bec il it y	im be cil i ty
im it ate	im i tate
im it a tion	im i ta tion
im mat ure	im ma ture
im mem or i,al	im me mo ri al
im men sit y	im men si ty
im mig rant	im mi grant
im min ent	im mi nent
im mor al it y	im mo ral i ty
im mor tal it y	im mor tal i ty
im mu nit y	im mu ni ty
im mu tab le	im mu ta ble
im ped im ent	im ped i ment
im pen et rab le	im pen e tra ble
im pen it ent	im pen i tent
im per at ive	im per a tive
im per cep tib le	im per cep ti ble
im per tin ent	im per ti nent
im pet us	im pe tus
im plac ab le	im pla ca ble
im plem ent	im ple ment
im plic ate	im pli cate
im plic a tion	im pli ca tion

im prac tic al	im prac ti cal
im preg nab le	im preg na ble
im prob ab le	im prob a ble
im pro pri et y	im pro pri e ty
im prov id ent	im prov i dent
im pu nit y	im pu ni ty
im pu rit y	im pu ri ty
in ab il it y	in a bil i ty
in ac ces sib le	in ac ces si ble
in ad vi sab le	in ad vis a ble
in an im ate	in an i mate
in ap tit ude	in ap ti tude
in aud ib le	in au di ble
in aus pic ious	in aus pi cious
in ca pab le	in ca pa ble
in cap ac it y	in ca pac i ty
in cid ence	in ci dence
in cis ion	in ci sion
in civ il it y	in ci vil i ty
in clin a tion	in cli na tion
in com par ab le	in com pa ra ble
in com pat ib le	in com pat i ble
in com pet ent	in com pe tent
in com pre hen sib le	in com pre hen si ble
in cor por ate	in cor po rate
in cor rig ib le	in cor ri gi ble

in cor rup tib le	in cor rupt i ble
in cred ib le	in cred i ble
in crim in ate	in crim i nate
in cu rab le	in cur a ble
in dec is ion	in de ci sion
in de fi nab le	in de fin a ble
in del ib le	in del i ble
in del ic ate	in del i cate
in dem nif y	in dem ni fy
in de struc tib le	in de struct i ble
in dic at ive	in dic a tive
in dic a tor	in di ca tor
in dig ent	in di gent
in di gest ib le	in di gest i ble
in dir ect	in di rect
in dis crim in ate	in dis crim i nate
in dis pen sab le	in dis pen sa ble
in div id u al	in di vid u al
in doc trin ate	in doc tri nate
in dom it ab le	in dom i tab le
in du bit ab le	in du bi ta ble
in ed ib le	in ed i ble
in ef fab le	in ef fa ble
in ef fic ien cy	in ef fi cien cy
in el ig ib le	in el i gi ble
in es ca pab le	in es cap a ble

in ev it ab le	in ev i ta ble
in ex cu sab le	in ex cus a ble
in ex or ab le	in ex o ra ble
in ex tric ab le	in ex tri ca ble
in fal lib le	in fal li ble
in fam y	in fa my
in fer i,or it y	in fe ri or i ty
in fid el	in fi del
in fin it es im al	in fin i tes i mal
in fin it y	in fin i ty
in firm ar y	in fir ma ry
in fir mit y	in fir mi ty
in flam mab le	in flam ma ble
in flex ib le	in flex i ble
in form at ive	in form a tive
in gen u it y	in ge nu i ty
in hab it ant	in hab i tant
in hos pit ab le	in hos pi ta ble
in im ic al	in im i cal
in im it ab le	in im i ta ble
in nu mer ab le	in nu mer a ble
in or din ate	in or di nate
in quis it ive	in quis i tive
in san it y	in san i ty
in scru tab le	in scru ta ble
in sec tic ide	in sect i cide

99

in se cu rit y	in se cu ri ty
in sen sib il it y	in sen si bil i ty
in si der	in sid er
in sig nif ic ant	in sig nif i cant
in spir a tion	in spi ra tion
in stab il it y	in sta bil i ty
in sub or din ate	in sub or di nate
in tan gib le	in tan gi ble
in teg ral	in te gral
in teg rit y	in teg ri ty
in tel lig ence	in tel li gence
in tel lig ib le	in tel li gi ble
in ten sif y	in ten si fy
in tim ac y	in ti ma cy
in tim id ate	in tim i date
in tox ic ant	in tox i cant
in tro duc tor y	in tro duc to ry
in val id ate	in val i date
in ven tor y	in ven to ry
in ver teb rate	in ver te brate
in ves tig ate	in ves ti gate
in vin cib le	in vin ci ble
in vit a tion	in vi ta tion
in vi ting	in vit ing
ir as cib le	i ras ci ble
ir id es cence	ir i des cence

ir rec on ci lab le	ir rec on cil a ble
ir rel ev ant	ir rel e vant
ir rig ate	ir ri gate
ir rit ant	ir ri tant

J

Jam ai ca	Ja mai ca
Jap an ese	Jap a nese
Jer u sal em	Je ru sa lem
jol lit y	jol li ty
ju bil ant	ju bi lant
ju dic i,al	ju di ci al
ju nip er	ju ni per
Ju pit er	Ju pi ter
jus tif i ab le	jus ti fi a ble
ju ven ile	ju ve nile

K

kim o no	ki mo no
kin et ic	ki net ic
kna ver y	knav er y
Kor e a	Ko re a

L

lab or at or y	lab o ra to ry
Lab rad or	Lab ra dor
lab yr inth	lab y rinth

lack ad ai sic al	lack a dai si cal
lac on ic	la con ic
la den	lad en
la ding	lad ing
lag oon	la goon
la it y	la i ty
lam ent	la ment
lap el	la pel
lar cen y	lar ce ny
las sit ude	las si tude
lat it ude	lat i tude
laud at or y	laud a to ry
lav at or y	lav a to ry
lax it y	lax i ty
Leb an on	Leb a non
leg ac y	leg a cy
le gal it y	le gal i ty
le ga tion	le ga tion
leg ib le	leg i ble
leg it im ac y	le git i ma cy
leg it im ate	le git i mate
leth ar gic	le thar gic
lex ic og raph er	lex i cog ra pher
lex ic on	lex i con
li ab il it y	li a bil i ty
lib er al it y	lib er al i ty

lig am ent	lig a ment
lig at ure	lig a ture
li ken	lik en
lim it a tion	lim i ta tion
liq uid ate	liq ui date
lit an y	lit a ny
lit er ac y	lit er a cy
lit er at ure	lit er a ture
lit ig a tion	lit a ga tion
li ner	lin er
lin im ent	lin i ment
li ning	lin ing
lin o le um	li no le um
liq uef y	liq ue fy
li ven	liv en
lo cal it y	lo cal i ty
log ar ithm	log a rithm
log ic al	log i cal
lon gev it y	lon gev i ty
lon git ude	lon gi tude
loo sen	loos en
lul lab y	lul la by
lum in ar y	lu mi nary
lu nac y	lu na cy
lu nat ic	lu na tic
lyr ic al	lyr i cal

mac ar o ni	mac a ro ni
mac ar oon	mac a roon
mach in a tion	mach i na tion
mac kin aw	mack i naw
mac kin tosh	mack in tosh
mad eir a	ma dei ra
Mad is on	Mad i son
mad rig al	mad ri gal
mag az ine	mag a zine
mag nam in it y	mag na nim i ty
mag nif ic ence	mag nif i cence
mag nif y	mag ni fy
mag nit ude	mag ni tude
main ten ance	main te nance
maj es tic	ma jest ic
maj or it y	ma jor i ty
ma ker	mak er
mal ad y	mal a dy
mal ev o lent	ma lev o lent
mal ig nant	ma lig nant
mal ig nit y	ma lig ni ty
mal in ger	ma lin ger
mal nu trit ion	mal nu tri tion

man ac le	man a cle
man dar in	man da rin
man dat or y	man da to ry
man eu ver	ma neu ver
man gan ese	man ga nese
man ic ure	man i cure
man if est	man i fest
man if old	man i fold
man ip u late	ma nip u late
man ure	ma nure
mar ath on	mar a thon
mar gar ine	mar ga rine
mar in er	mar i ner
mar it al	mar i tal
mar it ime	mar i time
mar mal ade	mar ma lade
mar oon	ma roon
mar tin et	mar ti net
mas tic ate	mas ti cate
mat ern al	ma tern al
math em at ics	math e mat i cal
mat ric u late	ma tric u late
mat rim o ny	mat ri mo ny
mat ure	ma ture
mat ur it y	ma tu ri ty
max im um	max i mum

mech an ic	me chan ic
med ic al	med i cal
med it ate	med i tate
mel o dram a	mel o dra ma
mem or an dum	mem o ran dum
mem or ize	mem o rize
mem or y	mem o ry
men dic ant	men di cant
men tal it y	men tal i ty
mer cen ar y	mer ce nar y
mer cif ul	mer ci ful
mer cil ess	mer ci less
mer id ian	me rid i an
mer it or ious	mer i to ri ous
mer rim ent	mer ri ment
met ab o lism	me tab o lism
met ic u lous	me tic u lous
met ric al	met ri cal
met ro pol it an	met ro pol i tan
mez zan ine	mez za nine
mi crom et er	mi crom e ter
mi grat or y	mi gra to ry
mil it ant	mil i tant
mi ner	min er
min im ize	min i mize
mi nor it y	min or i ty

mir ac le	mir a cle
mir ac u lous	mi rac u lous
mir age	mi rage
mis er ab le	mis er a ble
mis ta ken	mis tak en
mod ic um	mod i cum
mod if ic a tion	mod i fi ca tion
mof if y	mod i fy
mol ec ule	mol e cule
mol if y	mol li fy
mo men tar il y	mo men tar i ly
mon et ar y	mon e tar y
mon it or	mon i tor
mon oc le	mon o cle
mon og am y	mo nog a my
mon op o list	mo nop o list
mon ot on ous	mo not o nous
mon stros it y	mon stros i ty
mor al it y	mo ral i ty
mor at or i,um	mor a to ri um
mor tic ian	mor ti cian
mor tif y	mor ti fy
mo tiv ate	mo ti vate
mu cil age	mu ci lage
mul tip lic a tion	mul ti plic a tion
mu nic ip al	mu ni ci pal

mu nic ip al it y	mu nic i pal i ty
mu nif ic ent	mu nif i cent
mu nit ion	mu ni tion
mu sic al	mu si cal
mu tab le	mu ta ble
mu til ate	mu ti late
mu tin eer	mu ti neer
mu tin ous	mu ti nous
mu tin y	mu ti ny
mys tic al	mys ti cal

N

nat ion al it y	na tion al i ty
nat iv it y	na tiv i ty
nau tic al	nau ti cal
nav ig ab le	nav i ga ble
nav ig a tion	nav i ga tion
Neb ras ka	Na bras ka
nec es sit ate	nec es si tate
neg ate	ne gate
neg lig ib le	neg li gi ble
nem es is	nem e sis
neu tral it y	neu tral i ty
ni cet y	ni ce ty
nit ric acid	ni tric acid

no bil it y	no bil i ty
nom in al	nom i nal
non en tit y	non en ti ty
no ted	not ed
no tor i et y	no to ri e ty
nu mer ic al	nu mer i cal
nu trit ion	nu tri tion

O

ob jec tion ab le	ob jec tion a ble
ob lig ate	ob li gate
ob lig a tion	ob li ga tion
o b li ging	o blig ing
ob stac le	ob sta cle
ob stin ate	ob sti nate
oc cid ent	oc ci dent
oc tag on	oc ta gon
oc to gen ar i,an	oc to ge nar i an
od dit y	odd i ty
of fic ial	of fi cial
ol fac tor y	ol fac to ry
ol ig ar chy	ol i gar chy
om el et	om e let
om in ous	om i nous
om nib us	om ni bus

pach yd erm	pach y derm
pac if ic	pa cif ic
pac if ic a tion	pac i fi ca tion
paj am as	pa ja mas
pal at ab le	pal at a ble
pal av er	pa lav er
pal is ade	pal i sade
pal pab le	pal pa ble
Pan am a	Pan a ma
pan dem o nium	pan de mo ni um
pa pac y	pa pa cy
par ab le	par a ble
par ad ise	par a dise
par ad ox	par a dox
par ag raph	par a graph
par al ys is	pa ral y sis
par am ount	par a mount
par ap et	par a pet
par aph er nal i,a	par a pher nal i a
par ap le gia	par a ple gi a
par as ite	par a site
par as ol	par a sol
par en thes is	pa ren the sis

par it y	par i ty
par tic ip ant	par tic i pant
pat ern al	pa ter nal
path ol o gy	pa thol o gy
pat ric ian	pa tri cian
pat rim o ny	pat ri mo ny
pat rol man	pa trol man
pav il ion	pa vil ion
pec tor al	pec to ral
pec u liar	pe cu liar
pec u niar y	pe cu ni ar y
pe diat rics	pe di at rics
ped ig ree	ped i gree
pel ic an	pel i can
pen it ent	pen i tent
pen tag on	pen ta gon
per em tor y	per emp to ry
per fid y	per fi dy
per for ate	per fo rate
per func tor y	per func to ry
per im et er	pe rim e ter
per iph ery	pe riph er y
per is cope	per i scope
per it on i tis	per i to ni tis
per man ent	per ma nent
per mis sib le	per mis si ble

per pet rate	per pe trate
per pet u it y	per pe tu i ty
per plex it y	per plex i ty
per son al it y	per son al i ty
pes til ent	pes ti lent
pet rif y	pet ri fy
pet ro le um	pe tro le um
phan tas y	phan ta sy
pharm ac eu tics	phar ma ceu tics
phar mac ol o gy	phar ma col o gy
phen om en on	phe nom e non
phil an thro py	phi lan thro py
phil o soph ic al	phil o soph i cal
phon et ics	pho net ics
pho tog raph y	pho tog ra phy
phys ic al	phys i cal
phys iog no my	phys i og no my
pick an in ny	pick a nin y
pil lor y	pil lo ry
pim en to	pi men to
pin nac le	pin na cle
pi on eer	pi o neer
pi rac y	pi ra cy
pit if ul	pit i ful
pleb e ian	ple be ian
pleb is cite	pleb i scite

113

pleu ris y	pleu ri sy
por tic o	por ti co
pon tif ic al	pon tif i cal
pop u lar it y	pop u lar i ty
plu ral it y	plu ral i ty
pol ic y	pol i cy
po lit ic al	po lit i cal
pol it y	pol i ty
po lyg am y	po lyg a my
pos sib il it y	pos si bil i ty
pos ter it y	pos ter i ty
prac tic ab le	prac ti ca ble
pre cip it a tion	pre cip i ta tion
pred at or y	pred a to ry
pre dom in ant	pre dom i nant
pre em in ent	pre em i nent
pre fab ric ate	pre fab ri cate
pre lim in ary	pre lim i nar y
pre mat ure	pre ma ture
pre var ic ate	pre var i cate
prim ad on na	pri ma don na
pri mar il y	pri ma ri ly
pri mar y	pri ma ry
prim it ive	prim i tive
prin cip al	prin ci pal
pri or it y	pri or i ty

pri vac y	pri va cy
priv il ege	priv i lege
pro bit y	pro bi ty
proc lam a tion	proc la ma tion
prof lig ate	prof li gate
pro gen it or	pro gen i tor
pro let ar ian	pro le tar i an
prom en ade	prom e nade
prom in ent	prom i nent
prom is sor y	prom is so ry
pro pen sit y	pro pen si ty
proph ec y	proph e cy
pro po sal	pro pos al
pro pri et ar y	pro pri e tar y
pros el yte	pros e lyte
pros per it y	pros per i ty
prov id en tial	prov i den tial
pro vi ding	pro vid ing
prox im it y	prox im it y
pub lic ist	pub li cist
pu gil ism	pu gi lism
pul mon ar y	pul mo nar y
pu nit ive	pu ni tive
pur gat or y	pur ga tor y
pu rif y	pu ri fy
pu rit an	pu ri tan

pu rit y	pu ri ty
pu sil lan im ous	pu sil lan i mous
pyr am id	pyr a mid
Pyr en ees	Pyr e nees

Q

quad rille	qua drille
quad rup let	quad ru plet
Qua ker	Quak er
qual if ic a tion	qual i fi ca tion
quan dar y	quan da ry
qui et ude	qui e tude
quin tup let	quin tu plet
quiz zic al	quiz zi cal
quo rum	quor um

R

ra cy	rac y
rag am uf an	rag a muf an
Raj ah	Ra jah
rar it y	rar i ty
rat if y	rat i fy
ra ting	rat ing
rat ion al	ra tion al
re al it y	re al i ty

116

rea son ab le	rea son a ble
re cal cit rant	re cal ci trant
re cap it u late	re ca pit u late
re cep tac le	re cep ta cle
rec ip e	rec i pe
rec ip roc it y	rec i proc i ty
re ci tal	re cit al
rec it a tion	rec i ta tion
rec og nit ion	rec og ni tion
re crim in ate	re crim i nate
rec tif y	rec ti fy
rec tit ude	rec ti tude
rec tor y	rec to ry
red ol ent	red o lent
re fec tor y	rec fec to ry
re fi ner y	re fin er y
re for mat or y	re form a tory
re frac tor y	re frac to ry
reg im en	reg i men
reg im ent	reg i ment
re hab il it ate	re ha bil i tate
re ju ven ate	re ju ve nate
rel at ive	rel a tive
rel at iv it y	rel a tiv i ty
rel eg ate	rel e gate
rel ev ent	rel e vent

re li ab le	re li a ble
re lig ion	re li gion
re mar kab le	re mark a ble
rem ed y	rem e dy
rem in isce	rem i nisce
rep ar a tion	rep a ra tion
re pea ted	re peat ed
rep et it ion	rep e ti tion
rep lic a	rep li ca
re pos it or y	re pos i to ry
rep re sen tat ive	rep re sen ta tive
rep rim and	rep ri mand
re pri sal	re pris al
re pub lic an	re pub li can
rep u tab le	rep u ta ble
res id ence	res i dence
res id ue	res i due
res il ient	re sil ient
re spec tab le	re spect a ble
res pir a tion	res pi ra tion
re spon sib il it y	re spon si bil i ty
re spon sib le	re spon si ble
res tor a tion	res to ra tion
re stor at ive	re stor a tive
re sus cit ate	re sus ci tate
ret ic ent	ret i cent

ret in a	ret i na
ret in ue	ret i nue
re ti ring	re tir ing
ret rib u tion	ret ri bu tion
re u nion	re un ion
rev el a tion	rev e la tion
rev en ue	rev e nue
re vi val	re viv al
re vol ver	re volv er
rhet or ic	rhet o ric
rheu mat ism	rheu ma tism
rib o fla vin	ri bo flav in
ri pen	rip en
ri der	rid er
rid ic ule	rid i cule
ro sar y	ro sa ry
ro sy	ros y
ro tar y	ro ta ry
ru dim ent	ru di ment
ru ling	rul ing
ru min ant	ru mi nant

S

sac char in	sac cha rin
sac ram ent	sac ra ment

119

sac rif ice	sac ri fice
sac ril ege	sac ri lege
sag a	sa ga
sag a cious	sa ga cious
sag am ore	sag a more
sal am an der	sal a man der
sal ar y	sal a ry
sal i va	sa li va
sal on	sa lon
sal oon	sa loon
sal ute	sa lute
san at or ium	san a to ri um
sanc tif y	sanc t i fy
sanc tim o nious	sanc ti mo ni ous
sanc tif y	sanc ti fy
sand pi per	sand pip er
san guin ar y	san gui nar y
san it ar ium	san i tar i um
san it ar y	san i tar y
san it y	san i ty
sar coph ag us	sar coph a gus
sar sap ar il la	sar sa pa ril la
sas saf ras	sas sa fras
sav ant	sa vant
sa vior	sav ior
sce nar io	sce na ri o

scim it ar	scim i tar
scru tin y	scru ti ny
seb a ceous	se ba ceous
sec on dar y	sec ond ar y
sec ret ar y	sec re tar y
se cu rit y	se cu ri ty
sed im ent	sed i ment
sed it ion	sed di tion
sem in ar y	sem i nar y
sen at or	sen a tor
sen sib il it y	sen si bil i ty
sen tim en tal	sen ti men tal
sep ar a tor	sep a ra tor
ser en ade	ser e nade
ser ene	se rene
ser vit ude	ser vi tude
ses am e	ses a me
sev ere	se vere
sha ding	shad ing
sha ker	shak er
sha ving	shav ing
shi ny	shin y
sig nat ure	sig na ture
sig nif y	sig ni fy
sil age	si lage
sil ic a	sil i ca

sil ic ate	sil i cate
sil ic on	sil i con
sim il ar	sim i lar
sim il e	sim i le
sim il it ude	si mil i tude
sim plic it y	sim pli c i ty
sir oc co	si roc co
si zab le	siz a ble
skel et on	skel e ton
skep tic ism	skep ti cism
sky scra per	sky scrap er
sla ver	slav er
sla vish	slav ish
so lic it or	so lic i tor
so lic it ude	so lic i tude
sol id ar it y	sol i dar i ty
so lid if y	so lid i fy
sol it ar y	sol i tar y
so ror it y	so ror i ty
spec ial	spe cial
spec if ic a tion	spec i fi ca tion
spec if y	spec i fy
spec im en	spec i men

tab oo	ta boo
tac it turn	tac i turn
taf fet a	taf fe ta
ta king	tak ing
talk at ive	talk a tive
tan ger ine	tan ge rine
tan gib le	tan gi ble
tan tal ize	tan ta lize
tan tam ount	tan ta mount
tar an tu la	ta ran tu la
ta sty	tast y
tax a tion	tax a tion
tech nic al	tech ni cal
tech nic al it y	tech ni cal i ty
tech nic ian	tech ni cian
tech nic ol or	tech ni col or
tel ec ast	tel e cast
tel eg ram	tel e gram
tel eg raph	tel e graph
tel eg raph y	te leg ra phy
tel ep ath y	te lep a thy
tel eph one	tel e phone
tel es cope	tel e scope

tel ev ise	tel e vise
tel ev is ion	tel e vi sion
tem er it y	te mer i ty
tem per am ent	tem per a ment
tem per at ure	tem per a ture
tem por al	tem po ral
tem por ar y	tem po rar y
tem por ize	tem po rize
ten ab le	ten a ble
ten a cious	te na cious
ten ac it y	te nac i ty
ten em ent	ten e ment
ten tac le	ten ta cle
ten tat ive	ten ta tive
ter min al	ter mi nal
ter min ol o gy	ter mi nol o gy
ter min us	ter mi nus
ter ram y cin	ter ra my cin
ter rap in	ter ra pin
ter rib le	ter ri ble
ter rif y	ter ri fy
ter rit or ial	ter ri tor ri al
ter rit or y	ter ri to ry
tes tam ent	tes ta ment
tes tif y	tes ti fy
tes tim o nial	tes ti mo ni al

124

tes tim o ny	tes ti mo ny
tet an us	tet a nus
the at ric al	the at ri cal
the ol o gian	the o lo gian
the or em	the o rem
the or et ic al	the o ret i cal
the or ize	the o rize
the or y	the o ry
ther ap y	ther a py
ther mom et er	ther mom e ter
thes au rus	the sau rus
thrif ty	thrift y
ti dal	tid al
tim id it y	ti mid i ty
ti ming	tim ing
tog eth er	to geth er
ton sil lec to my	ton sil lec to my
top og raph y	to pog ra phy
to tal it ar ian	to tal i tar i an
to tal it y	to tal i ty
tour nam ent	tour na ment
trac tab le	trac ta ble
trad it ion	tra di tion
trag e dian	tra ge di an
trag ed y	trag e dy
tran quil it y	tran quil it y

trans con tin en tal	trans con ti nen tal
tran sit ion	tran si tion
tran sit ive	tran si tive
tran sit or y	tran si to ry
treb le	tre ble
trem en dous	tre men dous
trich in o sis	trich i no sis
trig on om et ry	trig o nom e try
Trin id ad	Trin i dad
trip lic ate	trip li cate
tri um vir ate	tri um vi rate
tu bing	tub ing
tu it ion	tu i tion
tur pit ude	tur pi tude
tu tel age	tu te lage
tym pan um	tym pa num
typ ic al	typ i cal
typ if y	typ i fy
ty pog raph y	ty pog ra phy
tyr an nic al	ty ran ni cal

U

ul ter ior	ul te ri or
ul tim ate	ul ti mate
ul tim a tum	ul ti ma tum
un ac coun tab le	un ac count a ble

126

un-Am er ic an	un-Am er i can
u nan im it y	u na nim i ty
u nan im ous	u nan i mous
un as su ming	un as sum ing
un at ten ded	un at tend ed
un av oid ab le	un a void a ble
un aw are	un a ware
un con dit ion al	un con di tion al
un con stit u tion al	un con sti tu tion al
u nic orn	u ni corn
u nif ic a tion	u ni fi ca tion
u nif orm	u ni form
u nif orm it y	u no form i ty
un so phis tic a ted	un so phis ti cat ed
un ti ring	un tir ing
up hea val	up heav al
u ra nium	u ra ni um
u sab le	u sa ble
u sage	us age
u til it ar ian	u til i tar i an
u til it y	u til i ty

V

vac cin ate	vac ci nate
vac u it y	va cu i ty
vag ab ond	vag a bond

val ed ic tor y	val e dic to ry
val id it y	va lid i ty
val u ab le	val u a ble
van il la	va nil la
van it y	van i ty
var i et y	va ri et y
Vat ic an	Vat i can
vau dev ille	vau de ville
veg et ab le	veg e ta ble
veg et ar i,an	veg e tar i an
veg et a tion	veg e ta tion
ve hem ent	ve he ment
ve hic le	ve hi cle
vel oc it y	vel oc i ty
ven er ab le	ven er a ble
ven is on	ven i son
ven til ate	ven ti late
ven til a tion	ven ti la tion
ven til a tor	ven ti la tor
ven tric le	ven tri cle
ver a cious	vex a cious
ver ac it y	ve rac i ty
ver an da	ve ran da
ver if ic a tion	ver i fi ca tion
ver if y	ver i fy
ver it ab le	ver i ta ble

ver it y	ver i ty
ver sat ile	ver sa tile
ver sif y	ver si fy
ver teb ra	ver te bra
ver tic al	ver ti cal
ves tib ule	ves ti bule
vet er in ar i,an	vet er i nar i an
vic in it y	vi cin i ty
vic is sit ude	vi cis si tude
vic tor ian	vic to ri an
vic tor y	vic to ry
vig il ance	vig i lance
vig i lant	vig i lant
vin eg ar	vin e gar
vir gin it y	vir gin i ty
vis cos it y	vis cos i ty
vis ib il it y	vis i bil i ty
vis ib le	vis i ble
vis ion ar y	vi sion ar y
vis it or	vis i tor
vi tal it y	vi tal i ty
vi tam in	vi ta min
viv ac it y	vi vac i ty
viv is ec tion	viv i sec tion
vol at ile	vol a tile
vo lu min ous	vo lu mi nous

vo tar y   vo ta ry

vul gar it y   vul gar i ty

vul ner ab le   vul ner a ble

W

wa ken   wak en

war il y   war i ly

wat er   wa ter

Wat er loo   Wa ter loo

whim sic al   whim si cal

whi ten   whit en

wi den   wid en

wi ly   wil y

wi ring   wir ing

wi ry   wir y

wit tic ism   wit ti cism

wri ter   writ er

wri ting   writ ing

Z

zep pel in   zep pe lin

zo o log ic al   zo o log i cal